Green Pastures

A Collection of

Devotionals, Testimonies, and Reflections

Green Pastures

A Collection of

Devotionals, Testimonies, and Reflections

Second Baptist Church Christian Writers Ministry

Roselle, New Jersey 07203

Rosetta Jamieson-Thomas, Editor

iUniverse, Inc.

New York   Bloomington

Green Pastures
A Collection of Devotionals, Testimonies, and Reflections

iUniverse books may be ordered through booksellers or by contacting:

iUniverse
1663 Liberty Drive
Bloomington, IN 47403
www.iuniverse.com
1-800-Authors (1-800-288-4677)

ISBN: 978-1-4401-9570-9 (sc)
ISBN: 978-1-4401-9571-6 (ebook)

Printed in the United States of America

iUniverse rev. date: 12/15/09

Endorsement

Green Pastures: A Collection of Devotionals, Testimonies and Reflections

Green Pastures is an inspiring work! By listening to the collective heartbeat of one local congregation, this book provides all of us with a practical, thoughtful, Christian perspective for our daily living. The contributing writers courageously confront the ups and downs of the human experience. This is an awesome offering that celebrates our awesome God!

Editor Rosetta Jamieson-Thomas has creatively compiled a significant collection of devotionals, testimonies and reflections that share the faith stories of the historic Second Baptist Church, Roselle, N.J.

In nine chapters, Jamieson-Thomas has woven together writings that address such topics as God's greatness, providential promises, relationships, faith, service, thanksgiving and prayer. It's worth noting that this is an intergenerational collaboration -- with the writers representing all stages of life and faith development.

As a pastor, Christian educator, and former area minister with *American Baptist Churches of New Jersey*, I know ***Green Pastures*** can be an invaluable resource for individuals, congregations, Bible study groups and church school classes that are serious about spiritual growth.

Glenn E. Porter, D.Min., Senior Pastor
Queen Street Baptist Church
Norfolk, VA

Acknowledgements

SBC Christian Writers Ministry is grateful to everyone who has contributed, in any way, to this publication. It is our hope that you have been blessed as you wrote, that you will be blessed as you read what others have written, and that your writing will be a blessing to others.

SBC Christian Writers Ministry extends very special thanks and our deepest appreciation to Reverend Dr. Glenn E. Porter, former Area Minister with American Baptist Churches of New Jersey, and current Senior Pastor of Queen Street Baptist Church, Norfolk, Virginia. We are grateful to Dr. Porter for having taken time out of his busy schedule to read, review and endorse this publication.

To all the following contributing writers, SBC Christian Writers Ministry says, **Write on!**

Contributing Writers

Reverend James E. Moore, Sr. Pastor
First Lady Minister Margaret Moore
Reverend Dr. Mollie Davis, Assistant Pastor
Reverend Barbara D. Turner, Assistant Pastor
Minister James E. Moore, Jr.
Minister Michael W. Tyree
Minister Alexis Hardy
Evangelist Deborah Hardy
Evangelist Marilyn Poole
Deacon Edward Mack
Deacon Billy McDowell
Deaconess Catherine Williams
Trustee Ricardo Carty
Barbara Briggs Turner
Vicie Carter

Annie Alexis Carty
Shauna M. Carty
Ayesha Z. Howard
Rosetta Jamieson-Thomas
Jennifer R. Jones
Linda McQuilla-Jones
Jubair LeGrand
Marette A. Moore
Marissa A. Moore
Yonette Morrison
Ruth Skerritt-Abraham
Joseph Thompson
Evonne Tyree

CLIMB Ministry

Kendrick Abraham
Dante Booker
Zachary Bragg
Asa Brewster
Ann-Marie Dickerson
John Mathews
Michael McDowell
Mindy Montgomery
Chelsea Monfort
Kareen Nazaire
Briana Thomas
Issac Thomas
Rupert Thomas
Alaina Thorne
Julian Sampson

This book is dedicated to the honor and glory of our Lord and Savior Jesus Christ, to Second Baptist Church Family, and to everyone who believes in the power of prayer and wants to strengthen his / her relationship with God — to grow in grace and experience the fullness of His blessings.

Table of Contents

.

Foreword

When Rosetta Jamieson-Thomas, Editor of *Green Pastures* asked me to write the foreword of this collection of devotionals, testimonies, and reflections, I was immediately humbled by the fact that I was being entrusted with the awesome responsibility of touting the value of this published work; not only to those who are in local proximity to our church, but to people all over the world. As pastor of a small congregation of more than four hundred members, I must say that I am thankful to Jesus Christ for this opportunity to represent Him in whatever capacity He affords me.

This published work is unique in the sense that the contributing authors range from an eight year old child, to former editors of local newspapers and published authors. What is even more honorable is that all but two authors of this book are members of Second Baptist Church, Roselle, N.J., of whom I am privileged to be their pastor.

As a pastor, responsible for the safe-keeping of the souls that God has entrusted to our care, I often ask myself, "Lord, are the people really grasping the messages and teachings that we labor to share with them, day-to-day, week-to-week, sermon after sermon?" It was when I read this precious collection of writings that my heart was warmed to discover that, "Yes Lord, they did receive the message! Yes Lord, they were listening!" The words of sermons and bible study lessons that I had prepared to inspire and encourage the congregation in the Lord, are now inspiring and encouraging me. It was then that I realized, in a fuller sense, what Jesus meant in Luke 6:38 when He said "Give, and it shall be given unto you; good measure, pressed down, shaken together, and running over, shall men give into your bosom. For with the same measure that ye mete withal it shall be measured to you again."

My prayer for the readers of this devotional is that your heart will be warmed and encouraged to desire more and more of Jesus Christ, as my heart has just become.

Your Humble Servant in Christ Jesus,
Pastor James E. Moore, Sr.
Second Baptist Church
Roselle, New Jersey, 07203

Introduction

But these things are written so that we may continue to believe that Jesus is the Messiah, the Son of God, and by believing on Him you will have life by the power of His name.

-John 20:31 (NLT)

The Second Baptist Church Christian Writers Ministry started in November 2005. The members of this group are individuals who are interested in writing as a ministry. Our mission as writers is to spread the gospel through the written word. The group meets once a month and the primary purpose of our meeting is to support, inspire and encourage one another. Our discussions focus on the art and craft of writing for publication, determining audience, and keeping abreast of trends in the Christian writers' market. Members' writing interests include all genres: novels, short stories, devotionals, articles, poetry and plays.

You do not have to be a professional writer or desire to be published to be a member of SBCC Writers' group. However, you must have an interest in writing, a personal relationship with God, knowledge of His Word, and a commitment to learning how to communicate His truths through writing.

As Christian writers, we are ministers of the Gospel of Christ and we are dedicated

- *To continue to spread the gospel through the written word*
- *To inspire, instruct, support, and encourage Christians to write*
- *To give aspiring writers an outlet for their writings, and to encourage and support their efforts to become published authors*
- *To inform and uplift the church family, and provide support for other ministries, as needed*
- *To glorify God through our writings*

We are very blessed to be able to bring you this publication which is the joint effort of the Christian Writers group members and other members of our congregation. All funds generated by this project will go towards the youth and creative arts ministries of Second Baptist Church, 200 Locust Street, Roselle, New Jersey 07203.

Green Pastures offers devotional thoughts, testimonies and reflections drawn from the personal experiences of the writers, and validated by the Word of God. These thoughts, testimonies and reflections are shared with you with the confidence that God will use them to bless and inspire you as you seek a closer walk with Him, and a faith-empowering relationship with our LORD and Savior, Jesus Christ.

-Rosetta Jamieson-Thomas, Editor

Acknowledge God's Greatness

Psalm 8: 1- 9 NLT

O LORD, our Lord, your majestic name fills the earth!
Your glory is higher than the heavens
You taught children and infants to tell of your strength, silencing your
enemies and all who oppose you.

When I look at the night sky and see the works of your fingers— the moon
and star you set in place —
What are people that you should think about them, mere mortals that you
should care about them?

Yet you made them only a little lower than God, and crowned them with
glory and honor.
You gave them charge over everything you made, putting all things under
their authority— the flocks and the herds and all the wild animals, the
birds in the sky, the fish in the sea, and everything that swims in the ocean
currents.
O LORD, our Lord, your majestic name fills the earth!

Prayer Focus

We worship and praise you LORD because of who you are.

Our Awesome God

Read Psalm 34: 15 – 20

"Many are the afflictions of the righteous: but the LORD delivereth him out of them all. He keepeth all of his bones; not one of them is broken."

–Psalm 34: 19-20

It is very true that, although you may have read a verse of Scripture several times, there comes a day when it takes on an entirely different meaning in your life. Somehow, based on what you are going through at a particular time, the season is ripe for that verse to minister to your spirit in a special way.

I have repeated Psalm 34:19 many times, and I have listened to preachers expound on this topic numerous times. This year, after the company that I work for merged with another, and I was relocated to the other company's office location there was some uneasiness. The commute was longer and the territory was unfamiliar. The faces were not all friendly. I was the stranger in their midst. I decided to use this Psalm for my pillar of strength for each day so I posted it on my computer to include in devotion every morning.

That's when I rediscovered verse 20 of that chapter that emphasizes that the God that we serve can do exceedingly and abundantly above all that we can ask or think. The verse spoke to me to say; not only does he deliver us out of all of our troubles but how does he do it? "He keepeth all his (the righteous) bones; not one of them is broken." It's not what you do but how you do it that makes you a cut above the rest. We exalt our Awesome God.

Abba Father, inscribe in our hearts and bring it to our remembrance each day that you are the God of all flesh, and there is nothing too hard for you. In Jesus Name. Amen.

- Ruth Skerritt-Abraham

In the Beginning

Read Genesis 1, 2:1-3

And God said, "Let there be lights in the firmament of the heaven to divide the day from the night: and let them be for signs, and for seasons, and for days, and years."

-Exodus 1:14

I recently took a flight to South Carolina to attend my sister-in-law's wedding. Our family left at 4:00 a.m. for the airport. After going through the ordeal of checking our luggage and going through security we proceeded to our departing gate to board the airplane.

Soon we settled in our seats with the other passengers and the plane was ready to proceed to the runway for take off. I glanced outside my window as we sped down the runway and noticed the lights flashing by as we started to ascend into the dark skies. Once we reached a certain altitude I saw the sun over the horizon, and the darkness turned to light as we witness the dawn of the day.

Imagine the breathtaking experience of flying in the sky among the clouds, looking at the clear skies and the rising sun! As I looked down I could see the autumn trees entering a metamorphism of green to orange to red, and it hit me what a mighty God we serve. He created the Heavens and the Earth and the land and the sea and gave us signs for seasons, and for days and years.

Father God you are the great IAM, the creator of everything that is, that was, and that which is to come. All creation will bow down before you oh God for your handwriting is on the sky, the sun, the moon and the stars. Everything that has breath will praise the Lord.

What a Mighty God we serve!

-Edward Mack

How Big Is Our Uzziah?

Read Colossians 3:23-24.

In the year that king Uzziah died I saw also the LORD sitting upon a throne, high and lifted up, and his train filled the temple.

-Isaiah 6:1

Who or what do we exalt above God? Without even thinking, we would probably respond saying, "nothing" and "no one" because we are in church every time the door opens, we are very active, we pray often, and we are very religious. But did we ever stop to think that sometimes being dutiful can hinder the development of a relationship.

What is the motivation behind our duty? What is the subject of our prayers? It was Uzziah's duty to be a faithful servant to the King. It was his obligation to honor the King. But be ye cautioned, "Servants, obey in all things your masters according to the flesh; not with eye-service, as men-pleasers; but in singleness of heart, fearing God; And whatsoever ye do, do it heartily, as to the Lord, and not unto men." (Colossians 3:23-24.)

Let's put the objects of our respect and adoration in perspective. We honor and obey our parents but they are not the Master. God admonishes wives to submit to their husbands, and husbands to love their wives but he does not require that they exalt each other as God. He wants parents to train their children in the way that they should go, according to the ways of the Lord, but they are not our trophies. They are to be nurtured for service to the King of Kings. He encourages us to give honor to whom honor is due, and to give to "Caesar" what is rightly his, but we dare not make "Caesar" our idol.

The parent, the husband, the wife, the child, the earthly leader & "stuff" - all fall in line behind our Heavenly Father. Note that even Isaiah the prophet was distracted. He did not recognize the power and majesty of God until King Uzziah died.

Do we think that we are exempt as Christians? For where your treasure is there your heart is also. Remember, more important than our sacrificial service is our relationship with God.

Lord, help us to exalt you above everyone else and everything else in our lives, so that nothing is able to separate us from reciprocating your love.

-Ruth Skerritt-Abraham

* * * *

I no longer call you servants, because a servant does not know his master's business. Instead, I have called you friends, for everything that I learned from my Father I have made known to you.

John 15:15

You Are Not All That!

Read Genesis 1:1-2:25

And the Lord God formed man of the dust of the ground, and breathed into his nostrils the breath of life; and man became a living soul.

–Genesis 2:7

When you look at Genesis chapters 1 and 2 you see that in the beginning the Lord made the world and He made you. Now some people think that they are all that. But do they know that all they are is dust? I hope you do. And when you die, you're just going to turn back to dust, and hopefully go to heaven. So, don't think you're all that, because GOD IS!

Dear Lord, you made me and I will enjoy that life cheerfully.

You're not all that. GOD Is!

Annie Alexis Carty *(8 years old)*

* * * *

But Jesus called them (His disciples) unto him and said, "Let the little children come unto Me, and do not forbid then; for of such is the kingdom of God. Assuredly, I say to you, whoever does not receive the kingdom as a little child will by no means enter."

–Luke 18:16–17(NKJV)

One thing have I desired of the Lord, that I will seek after; that I may dwell in the house of the Lord all the days of my life, to behold the beauty of the Lord, and to enquire in His temple.

–Psalm 2:4

Nothing Can Compare to You, O Lord
-A Reflection

Read Psalm 113:5-9; 23:1-6

Who is like the Lord our God who dwells on high?

-Psalm 113:5

Who is like the Lord? Who never leaves nor forsakes me? Who is the Friend that sticks closer than a brother? Who never turns His back on me, even though I mess up over and over again? Who comforts me in my times of distress? Who lulls me to sleep with His peace that passes all understanding? Who guards my heart and mind? Who fills my empty cup with overflowing love, joy, peace, long suffering, gentleness, goodness, faith, meekness, and temperance? Who gives me the desires of my heart? Oh Lord, IT IS NOBODY BUT YOU!

You always supply my needs according to your glorious riches. You prepare tables before me in the presence of my enemies. My cup does run over. God, you are so good! My love for you is unmatched. With everything that I have I want to bless you. With my tongue I will bless you. With my actions I will bless you. In my involvement I will bless you. Even when I do not understand I will bless you. In EVERYTHING I will bless you.

You are the God of peace and love. Thank You, Heavenly Father. I always desire to be in your presence. As one song writer wrote, "just to know you in all your ways," that is what I long for. Even if I never know your ways, I will still continue to bless you, God. You are everything. You allow me to forget about myself and remind me to focus on you. I praise you for that.

One thing that I desire of you, Lord, is to please and to know you in all of your ways.

-Marette A. Moore

My Everything

Read Psalm 18: 1-3

For in Him we live and move and have our being.

-Acts 17:28 (KJV)

Magazines racks across the country are stacked with pictures of celebrities who bear visual appeal, and seemingly represent the longed for ideal image.

Image sells and people like to get an eyeful of that which tantalizes the senses. They often fall captive to the fairy tale concept of the perfect person, that is, the perfect man . . . the perfect woman . . . the perfect relationship — the whole package!

But in seeking some kind of emotional fulfillment in appearances alone, we miss the sweet fulfillment offered by the eternal, unseen God who longs to be our Everything. It is not until we understand His desire to encompass us completely, that we will experience fulfillment at its deepest level.

The Psalmist David wrote, "The Lord is my rock and my fortress, and my deliverer; my God, my strength in whom I will trust; my buckler, and the horn of my salvation, and my high tower." (Psalm 18:2). In essence, He is Everything to me.

When we get a glimpse of His perfection our eyes, minds, and longing spirit will be filled beyond measure with a healthy appreciation for the temporal, but more so with the wonder of the Eternal; that the Lord alone is our Everything.

Lord Jesus, thank you for being my Rock to stand upon; my Fortress to hide in; my Deliverer to bring me out; and my God. Truly, there's none beside you. Amen.

Time won't fade the image of God.

-Margaret Moore

Worshipper

Read Psalm 34

But the hour cometh, now is when the true worshippers shall worship The Father in spirit and in truth: for The Father seeketh such to worship Him.

-John 4:23

In Psalm 34, King David expressed his love for the Lord through worship. It was his response to the Lord's response towards David's heart cry, to his desperation, to his need. The hand of the Lord had delivered. . . . So King David worshipped.

The man at the Gate Beautiful was brought daily to "the gateway" to ask for an offering. At the gateway to the temple, Peter and John saw him, and Peter declared, "Silver and gold have I none, but such as I have, I give thee in the Name of Jesus Christ". Upon his healing, the man at the gateway worshipped.

The woman with the alabaster box poured the perfumed oil upon Jesus. She knew Him as a Deliverer, and her response was to worship. I dare say that Shadrach, Meshach, and Abednego worshipped God in their declarations. They refused to eat the king's meat, or bow at the sound of his music. Daniel positioned himself in the window, facing the Holy City, three times a day, in prayer. His response to God was worship.

As "lively stones" given to reasonable service, begin to worship. Pour your worship upon Jesus; declare His goodness; let nothing separate you from His love. The hour has come . . . worship!

-Barbara D. Turner

View from the Throne Room

Read Luke 18: 22-37

What is man, that thou art mindful of him; and the son of man, that thou visitest him?

–Psalm 8:4

The Bible tells us that God sits high and looks low. "Thus saith the LORD, The heaven is my throne, and the earth is my **footstool**: where is the house that ye build unto me? and where is the place of my rest?" When I envision these two scenes, I equate it to looking down at an ant's hill. I could hardly pick out the shade of one ant from another. The ants are busy scurrying and gathering stuff; going back and forth in some kind of organized chaos. In their minds there is organization, in my mind it is chaos. What if I had stepped on that ant hill? Only then would they notice me ... but at that time it would be too late. There would have already been casualties.

I believe that it is so with God. As He watches us going about our daily tasks, the majority of which has nothing to do with our service to Him, He has pity upon us. "And as it was in the days of Noah, so shall it be also in the days of the Son of man." (Luke 17:26) "Likewise also as it was in the days of Lot; they did eat, they drank, they bought, they sold, they planted, they builded;" (Luke 17:28). We are erecting buildings, and gathering "stuff" that we think we need. If God decides to just step down to get our attention we could all be crushed in an instant.

The scripture says "What is man, that thou art **mindful** of **him**; and the son of man, that thou visitest **him**? (Psalm 8:4) The reason being ... we are His Creation. He knows us by name. He has the very strands of hair on our heads numbered. Each one of us is special to Him.

Remember not to take his affection for granted. We must always recognize the sovereignty and power of our Maker and reverence Him. Always looking up making sure that we are doing what is pleasing in His sight, being mindful that God is still on the throne.

We thank you God for your grace that is sufficient for us and Your mercy that endureth forever. In Jesus Name Amen.

- Ruth Skerritt-Abraham

* * * *

Let us then approach the throne of grace with confidence, so that we may receive mercy and find grace to help us in our time of need.

Hebrew 4:16

"Amazed By His Grace"

(Quote taken from Pastor James King, Chicago Heights, IL)

"But the God of all grace, who hath called us unto his eternal glory by Christ Jesus, after that ye have suffered a while, make you perfect, stablish, strengthen, settle you."

-1 Peter 5:10

What is this thing called grace? Some say it is unmerited favor. In other words, it is something we receive whether or not we do something to get it. When I look at it, I see it as pardon, even though our actions deserve other consequences. With this latter definition, many have (myself included) taken advantage of the fact that God will bestow pardon upon us as we acknowledge our faultiness/faults. There have been plenty of times when I have performed some heinous acts that could have, and probably should have, resulted in my immediate death, (physical and spiritual), but my merciful God and Father chose to spare my life.

During those times, I was reminded that God's grace (was) sufficient for (me)…(as His) strength (was) made perfect in weakness." (2 Corinthians 12:9, in part) Yet even after I was given renewed life and had exchanged my weakness for God's strength, I went back and messed up in the same and sometimes even worse manner. During those moments, was I, in fact, taking advantage of grace? At the time, I may not have thought so, but after reflecting on my actions, I definitely acknowledged that I knowingly disobeyed God in order to satisfy my own desires of fulfillment. Why didn't God snuff me out then? Was more grace being bestowed upon me? If this was the case, I can truly and clearly see why grace is seen as amazing.

Who else but God would continue to show pardon and kindness to the likeness of disobedient and rebellious humanity? Of course God knows what the outcome of our lives will be…whether or not we will completely surrender our desires and will to Him or if we will be cut off finally for doing our own things. Perhaps God continues to give us chance after chance to get it right because He does not want us to be lost eternally. I am thankfully assured that this latter stance is the case. We must, however, mature in our actions, speech, and thoughts, living as if this is the last time we will receive God's grace. We must be intentional about living to constantly please God.

"Furthermore then we beseech you, brethren, and exhort you by the Lord Jesus, that as ye have received of us how ye ought to walk and to please God, so ye would abound more and more." (1 Thessalonians 4:1)

-Marette A. Moore

* * * *

And God is able to make all grace abound toward you; that ye, always having all sufficiency in all things, may abound to every good work:

2 Corinthian 9:8

For by grace you have been saved through faith, and that not of yourselves; it is the gift of God, not of works, lest anyone should boast.

Ephesians 2:8-9NKJV

And of His fullness we have all received, and grace for grace. For the law was given through Moses, but grace and truth came through Jesus Christ.

John 1: 16-17 NKJV

Stimulate and Grow Your Faith

Read Hebrews 11: 1-3; 12: 1-2

Faith is the confidence that what we hope for will actually happen: it gives us assurance about things we cannot see. Through their faith the people in the days of old earned a good reputation.

By faith we understand that the entire universe was formed by God's command, that what we now see did not come from anything that can be seen.

Therefore, since we are surrounded by such a huge crowd of witnesses to the life of faith, let us strip off every weight that slows us down, especially the sin that so easily trips us up. And let us run with endurance the race God has set before us. We do this by keeping our eyes on Jesus, the champion who initiates and perfects our faith.

Prayer Focus:

Ask God to increase your faith; make you a person who walks by faith and not by sight, and to give you the courage to stand on His promises, no matter what your circumstances are.

Where Is Your Faith?

Read Hebrews 11:1-3

Now faith is the substance of things hoped for, the evidence of things not seen.

-Hebrews 11:1

It always seems easy to tell someone who is going through a situation — to encourage them by saying, "just have faith in God, everything will be alright"— but when it's you who is in the situation, it is not so easy.

I was going through a health issue that might require surgery, and I was having negative thoughts —and even thoughts about death. I had to stop, check myself and question, "Where is my faith in God"? I started searching through the Bible for scriptures that would comfort me, and I was led to read Isaiah 41:10 *"Fear thou not; for I am with thee: be not dismayed; for I am thy God: I will strengthen thee; yea, I will help thee; yea I will uphold thee with the right hand of my righteousness."*

I surrendered myself over to the will of God, and said Lord, "Whatever is your will, I trust you." The morning before I went for testing, my daughter, Reverend Barbara Turner, laid hands on me anointing me with oil and prayed saying "it is already done!"

As I waited for testing, I continued to read my scripture and memorized it. I was calm and at peace. When the testing was over, the nurse said that I was lucky that I would not need surgery, only medication. I looked at the nurse and the doctor and said, "It's not luck. I am blessed. Thank God!"

I praise Him and give Him all the glory. Through faith, you too can experience His peace in your moments of crisis. Dare to believe God!

- Barbara Briggs Turner

Dead Faith

Read James 2:15-18

Even so faith, if it hath not works, is dead, being alone.

–James 2:17

To say, "I claim it by faith", does not necessarily mean you don't have to work hard to attain it. Far too often we expect to sit back and receive blessings without putting forth any effort. There are times when God will allow us to be blessed in a manner in which we will not have to extend ourselves.

However, we must realize that faith and works coincide with one another. Yes, God is at the root of all blessings, and our works are not what create those blessings. "Even so faith, if it hath not works, is dead, being alone." We cannot reach our goals or bless others without trying.

Lord God, as you continue to increase my faith, instruct me on how to increase my efforts. Hold me accountable to you Lord on keeping my works consistent with my faith in you. Make me realize daily that while you are the worker of miracles, I must continue to work at whatever you have purposed my hands to do. I do not want to misrepresent you by exhibiting laziness. Help me to become an example of a hard working servant of Christ. In the name of Jesus I pray, amen.

If our efforts and our attempts are not lining up with our faith, then our faith is nothing more than a wish. Exercise your faith; be a doer of the Word.

- Michael W. Tyree

The Good Shepherd

Read Psalm 23

But my God shall supply all your need according to His riches in glory by Christ Jesus.

–Philippians 4:19

Having learned Psalm 23 as a child, it has become engrained in my heart and manifested in my life over the years. It has been my testimony for as long as I can remember. During those times when it seemed I had nothing or that no one even cared, I remembered, "The Lord is My Shepherd; I shall not want."

Whether you've lost loved ones or possessions, whether your physical or mental health is being tried, or whether you're walking through what *seems* like Death Valley, remember that God is always with you and will always take care of you.

Don't lose hope. Keep the faith day by day knowing that the Good Shepherd will always take care of all your needs. Consequently, you will come to know and declare verse six daily: "Surely goodness and mercy shall follow me all the days of my life; and I will dwell in the house of the Lord for ever."

Father God, I thank and praise you for being my Shepherd and for taking care of all my needs today. Help me to continue to trust you every day of my life.

Jesus knows his sheep by name and they know his voice and follow him; they run from strangers for they know not their voices.

– Deborah Hardy

God Knows Economic Woes

Read Matthew 6:25-34

And my God shall supply all your need according to His riches in glory by Christ Jesus.

-Philippians 4:19(NKJV)

I was around 15 years old when my father lost his job. The impact was similar to what's happening to families affected by layoffs in America today. Losing his job back then meant there wasn't enough money to pay the rent for the house we lived in, and my mother's teacher's salary couldn't meet the needs of our family.

The downward spiral is fast and scary for a family when the primary breadwinner loses his or her job. Yet, it is when we are at our lowest that we often realize and accept the closeness of God. God made a way out of our economic woes. He provided my mother with a foothold in America, where she worked two full-time jobs concurrently to earn enough money to try to rescue her family. My brothers and I joined her and studied hard in school, and worked hard whenever we had a job opportunity. God blessed us with good health and opened doors. Sadly, my father and grandmother died in Jamaica.

Although it is difficult to feel secure when we don't know where our next paycheck is coming from, we can find reassurance in Matthew 6: 25 - 34. Jesus said, "Therefore I say to you, do not worry about your life, what you will eat or what you will drink; nor about your body, what you will put on. Is not life more than food and the body more than clothing? … For your heavenly Father knows that you need all these things. But seek first the kingdom of God and His righteousness and all these things shall be added to you."

God's grace is sufficient. Father, please lift up mine eyes to the hills from whence cometh my help.

- Shauna M. Carty

God IS...

Read Hebrews 11: 1 - 6

The fool has said in his heart, "There is no God."

- Psalm 53:1 NKJV

There are so many people walking around believing that there is no God. Often, they are the rich and pampered beneficiaries of the prayers others said for them and the blessings others earned. Rarely—if ever—does the poor and desperate person deny that God exists. They usually know God for themselves because they have cried out to Him when no one else could save them and He rescued them from death.

God exists. Talking to God in prayer and reading His Holy Word, the Bible, strengthen our faith. "But without faith it is impossible to please Him, for he who comes to God must believe that He is, and that He is a rewarder of those who diligently seek Him." Hebrews 11:6

Father, please make yourself real to us; help us to believe in You.

God loves us so much, He sent Jesus to die for us, even when we rejected Him.

- Ricardo and Shauna Carty

Victory Holds It Together

Read 2 Corinthians 2: 14-16

Now thanks be unto God, which always causeth us to triumph in Christ...

-2 Corinthians 2: 14a

No matter what the task, no matter what the situation, no matter how much we think we've lost or have been defeated throughout the week, still end your week in VICTORY. With Christ we win! There is no battle that's too great for us to win. It is Christ who empowers us.

Think of victory as bookends. When we start the week off in victory and close it out in victory, everything else in between stays in place because victory holds it together. When we exist in between victory's bookends through Jesus Christ, satan's chance of prolonging horrible weeks, months, and years are minimized. We are triumphant because of Christ, and as we triumph people will even be able to "smell" the savor of God's knowledge. "For we are to God the fragrance of Christ among those who are being saved and among those who are perishing." (2 Cor. 2:15 NKJV).

Declare the victory! ". . . be strong in the Lord, and in the power of His might." (Ephesians 6:10)

Lord Jesus, I thank you for suffering and dying for me, and for your victory over death. Thank you for the presence of the Holy Spirit in my life enabling me to triumph over the enemy and over adverse circumstances.

-James E. Moore, Jr.

Run with Endurance

Read Ephesians 6:10-18

"Put on the whole armor of God, that you may be able to stand against the wiles of the devil."

-Ephesians 6:11 NKJV

The Bible tells of a holy and righteous God who will one day judge us all, punish evildoers, and reward those who seek and serve Him. It warns that as the return of Jesus Christ approaches, evil in the world will increase.

I see evidence of this around me that strengthens my faith in God. A play called "Jesus 2000" has been performed internationally by Father Richard HoLung and Friends to raise funds for the organization Missionaries of the Poor, which provides services and love to the poor on the island of Jamaica and around the world. In the play, the devil, or satan, is seen lurking in the background awaiting the opportunity to spring into action and destroy. He is excited by misery.

To safeguard against this, I embrace the scripture: "Stand therefore, having girded your waist with truth, having put on the breastplate of righteousness, and having shod your feet with the preparation of the gospel of peace, above all, taking the shield of faith with which you will be able to quench the fiery darts of the wicked one. And take the helmet of salvation, and the sword of Spirit, which is the word of God." (Ephesians 6:14-17)

Father, please cover us with your whole armor.

The battle is the Lord's, and we already have the victory.

- Ricardo and Shauna Carty

The Divine Stimulus Package

Read 1 King 17: 8-16

And my God shall supply all your needs according to his riches in glory by Christ Jesus.

-Phil.4:19 (NKJV)

As I passed a news-stand on a street corner in New York City, this headline in one of the local newspapers caught my attention:

FIND THE UPSIDE IN THE DOWNTURN.

I picked up the paper and read the full page advertisement posted by an upscale New York educational institution seeking students for its graduate degree programs. It encouraged the reader to "think progression not recession" – to turn the current economic downswing into an opportunity — to find the pathway to success.

Today as we are faced with foreclosures, downsizing, bankruptcy, job-loss, and unemployment, where can we find prosperity —the upside of this recession? Is it in higher education as the advertisement suggests, in the President's Stimulus Package, or in God's promises?

Like the widow of Zarephath, have we come to the end of our resources? "I have not a cake, but an handful of meal in a barrel, and a little oil in a cruise: and, behold, I am gathering two sticks, that I may go in and dress it for me and my son, that we may eat it, and die," she told Elijah. Are we taking God at His word or are we ready to give up or to compromise our faith in God?

Our God promises to multiply our resources beyond our expectations. For thus says the Lord God of Israel: "The bin of flour shall not be used up, nor shall the jar of oil run dry, until the day the Lord sends rain on the earth." (1 Kings 17:14). The widow of Zarephath believed God's word spoken to her through Elijah. She obeyed God's words, and she received her miracle. Through a simple act of faith she found "the upside in her economic downturn."

God has given us the assurance that He will always meet our needs. No matter how hopeless our situation seems, God will sustain us. He will provide "exceedingly abundantly above all that we ask or think" (Ephesians 3:20) but we must believe His promises and act on our belief by obeying His Word. Then "the Lord will give us that which is good, and our land will yield its increase." (Psalm 85:12)

Use the challenges of the present economic situation as a stimulus to grow your faith in God, and "Let the Lord be magnified who has pleasure in the prosperity of His servants."

–Psalm 35:27

Blessed be the Lord who daily loads us with benefits, even the God of our salvation (Psalm 68:19). To Him be glory and honor, forever. Amen.

- Rosetta Jamieson-Thomas

* * * *

Look at the birds of the air, for they neither sow nor reap nor gather into barns: yet your heavenly Father feeds them. Are you not of more value than they? (Matthew 6:26 NKJV)

Poor in Possessions; Rich in Faith

Read James 2:5

"Remove far from me vanity and lies: give me neither poverty nor riches; feed me with food convenient for me: Lest I be full, and deny thee, and say, Who is the Lord? Or lest I be poor, and steal, and take the name of my God in vain."

–Proverbs 30:8-9

The richer a person is, the more likely he is to deny God.

As people advance socially, they tend to mentally exalt themselves to the level of God. Some deny His existence. Some think they don't need Him. Others reinvent Him.

Yet the Bible tells us that Jesus is the same today, yesterday, and forever (Hebrews 13:8). And contrary to society's custom of reserving the highest privilege for the rich, God has chosen to make the poor rich in faith. (See James 2:5)

"Blessed are the poor in spirit; for theirs is for the kingdom of heaven." Matthew 5:3

How great is your faith?

Father, please increase our faith in You.

- Ricardo and Shauna Carty

You Are Not Alone

Read John 14: 1-4

I will not leave you comfortless: I will come to you.

-John 14: 18

It appears to me that every time I hear someone talking, a loved one or someone they knew has passed on. Whether it's a relative, friend, loved one or a co-worker, no one can fully understand what that individual is going through. The thought of never seeing that person again, never talking or laughing with that person....Jesus understood this. In Chapter 14 of the Gospel of John, Jesus is comforting His disciples knowing that His time to do His Father's will is coming closer.

But He assured them that He would not leave them alone; that He would send them a Comforter. Sometimes when a person is grieving the time he wants to be alone is the time that the Comforter is helping him. That memory of what was, and the good times shared with that loved one, can bring enjoyment and peace to an individual.

Let us continue to pray for the family and friends that are grieving for a loved one, knowing that Jesus is preparing a place for them, and He is coming to receive them. They are truly blessed.

Father God, in the name of Jesus we trust and thank you that you are with those who are grieving, knowing that your Word said that you will never leave us or forsake us, and your Word will not return to you void.

Be still and know that I am God.

- **Edward Mack**

What's the Weather Forecast?

Read Mark 4:35-40

And he arose, and rebuked the wind, and said unto the sea, Peace, be still. And the wind ceased, and there was a great calm.

–Mark 4:39

Storms can be powerful or storms can be calm. Which one of these storms are you facing now? A quiet storm or one that will cause destruction? As Christians we go through different obstacles, and tests of our faith. There are certain obstacles that we should have never gone through, and there are others that will lead us to greater gain in Christ.

This brings me back to Peter's storm. He went through a testing of his faith and had his eyes on Christ. As soon as he focused on what could get the best of him he began to sink. But as soon as he put his eyes back in focus he reached the Master with no problem.

My brothers and sisters, how many times have we gone to the Lord and asked Him to help us through our storms, and when the going got tough we lost sight of Him? Re-focus your vision on Him! He wants to help us, He wants to lead us to Victory, but if we don't stay focused we will loose out on what blessings He intends for us.

What ever weather you're facing, keep your eyes on Jesus. He can pull you through.

–Marissa Moore

Stay True

Read Psalm 34: 1-10

I will bless the Lord at all times
His praise shall continually be in my mouth.

In all our trials and tribulations
Just stay true
In all our trials and tribulations
Have patience
In all our trials and tribulations
Wait on the LORD
He will bring you through
Just stay true.

Oh, taste and see that the LORD is good
Blessed is the man who trusts in Him.

Just stay true
Have patience
Wait on the LORD
And He will bring you through.

- Marilyn Poole

Stand on His Promises

Hebrews 10:22-24 (NKJV)

Let us draw near with a true heart in full assurance of faith, having our hearts sprinkled from an evil conscience, and our bodies washed with pure water.
Let us hold fast the profession of our faith without wavering; for He is faithful that promised: and let us consider one another to provoke to love and to good works.

From an Old Hymn

Standing on the promises that cannot fail,
When the howling storms of doubt and fear assail
By the living word of God I shall prevail
Standing on the promises of God

Prayer Focus

E. V. Hill stated, "When you lose from your memory banks what God has done, you will doubt what God will do."

Let us pray for courage to face tomorrow because of what God did yesterday; what He is doing today; and what He promises to do tomorrow.

Wings of an Eagle

Read Isaiah 40:28-31

But they that wait upon the LORD shall renew their strength; they shall mount up with wings as eagles; they shall run, and not be weary; and they shall walk, and not faint.

-Isaiah 40:31

I would like to share with you my parasailing experience in the Bahamas, and the feeling of being air-borne like a bird flying through the sky. This was my first time in the air without being on a plane and I admit it was an intense moment. As I left the docking pier and the boat accelerated to top speed to get me air-borne I began praying to God that I return to land safely and see my wife again. I also prayed that I didn't, all of a sudden, fall into the sea. Once I was air-borne I experienced a sense of jealousy and envy for the birds that do this naturally. I can testify that this experience really made me appreciate God's creation even more. At that height I saw the Bahamas from a different perspective.

The experience of feeling like a bird, away from all the hustle and confusion of the land—alone in the air with God and his creation—is awesome. I saw the mountains, the blue sea, and the different color roof tops of the houses below. As I soar high above I was filled with this awesome feeling of freedom—with not a worry in the world. All nervousness and fear was gone and I did not want to come down. I saw God's creation with out the aid of an air-plane. It brought a better understanding of Isaiah 40:31, "they shall mount up with wings as eagles". God is the source of our strength. When life gets you down, depend on His strength and you will rise high above your circumstances.

Cast all your worries unto Him and enjoy the sense of freedom that comes with trusting God.

- Edward Mack

Help Is On the Way

Read Psalm 121: 1-8

Let us therefore come boldly to the throne of grace, that we may obtain mercy and find grace to help us in time of need.

–Hebrews 4:16 NKJV

When nobody and nothing else can help, know that God will be your very present help in trouble. Don't just take your situation as the final answer. Psalm 121 gives us the assurance of God's help.

I will lift up my eyes unto the hills. From where does my help come?
My help comes from the Lord, who made heaven and earth.
He will not let your foot to be moved: he who keeps you will not slumber.
Behold, he who keeps Israel will neither slumber nor sleep.
The Lord is your keeper: the Lord is your shade on your right hand.
The sun will not strike you by day, nor the moon by night.
The Lord will keep you from all evil; he will keep your life.
The Lord will keep your going out and your coming in, from this time forth, and even for evermore. (ESV)

Don't give up. Look up. Help is on the way.

I thank you, Father God, for the hope and the assurance of your abiding presence with me, and for your protection by day and by night.

-James E. Moore, Jr.

Lifted From Low by Faith

Read Philippians 4:6-7

The Lord is near to those who have a broken heart and saves such as have a contrite spirit"

-Psalm 34:18 NKJV

How do you cope with the low moments in life? Some people get high on humor, hence the saying, "Laughter is good medicine." Some rely on other ways, like drugs and liquor, that promise a high or buzz, but lead to self-destruction.

I had a really low moment recently when depression caught me by surprise. Everything was well enough in my world, but beyond my little nucleus, tragedy had struck. First, I heard about a mother in New York who'd killed her three children. Then, I found out that my friend's eleven-year-old niece had committed suicide. At the same time, I was reporting a story about a nineteen-year-old college student who had been murdered.

As I cried, I began to sing songs of praise to God. Eventually, God began to comfort me with His word. Bible verses I had read so many times that they were etched in my memory came to mind: "… there is a friend who sticks closer than a brother." (Proverbs 18:24) "Casting all your cares on Him; for He cares for you." (1 Peter 5:7) Gradually, God restored my peace and filled me with His joy. My circumstances hadn't changed, but the low I was wallowing in had been lifted—praise God in Jesus' name!

No matter how unbearable it seems, God has the power to lift us out of the lowest places in our lives. "…weeping may endure for a night, but joy comes in the morning." (Psalm 30:5).

Father, please comfort and keep us until You restore our joy.

- Ricardo and Shauna Carty

Pay Day Is Coming

Read Job 42: 10-12

So the Lord blessed the latter end of Job more than his beginning. . .

-Job 42: 10 & 12a

God promised that He would never leave us nor forsake us. So why does it seem that often times He has! The enemy wants us as believers to doubt that God will come through for us. In actuality though, the Father is near us even more. If we doubt in our minds we are saying, "God I don't trust you." This is a dangerous predicament to be in.

As a young Christian, I have had many times of doubt in my mind, but I know that this means that I'm not putting my trust in God. "Put your trust in God" is not just a cute phrase that is passed along in Church, but is something that needs to be applied. We must trust Him even when we don't see the victory on the other side. If I would have given up on school I would not have received the promise of graduation. If I would have given up on work, I would not have received favor on a job that people have quit. I would also be out of a pay check! If we give in and just give up your pay day and mine will never come. So today make it your personal mission to continue on, because payday is coming.

So let's not get tired of doing what is good. At just the right time we will reap a harvest of blessing if we don't give up. (Galatians 6:9 NLT)

-Marissa Moore

What's Lacking?

Read James 1:4-6

If any of you lack wisdom, let him ask of God, that giveth to all men liberally, and upbraideth not; and it shall be given him.

–James 1:5

Have there been times in your life that you felt you were lacking something? Was it wisdom? You know that the Lord said He would help us if this is what we need. In your mind I know you are saying, yes that's me. I had no idea what to do in this situation, so I asked this or that person. Or just maybe you tried to keep it to yourself.

If you are still bumping your head against a wall and getting nowhere, ask God. He is a Big God, but He makes time for us because He's concerned about us. God knows what we go through before we go through it, but He wants to see if we will turn to Him. He never "bum-rushes" us. He waits patiently for us to ask. So today, ask Him to supply whatever you are lacking; ask of Him and gain knowledge from Him.

My God shall supply all your need according to His riches in glory by Christ Jesus. Now unto God and our Father be glory for ever and ever. (Philippians 4:19-20)

-Marissa Moore

Equipment for the Journey

Read Joshua 1: 1-8

This Book of the Law shall not depart from your mouth, but you shall meditate in it day and night, that you may observe to do according to all that is written in it.

-Joshua 1:8a NKJV

I heard a story about a Christian traveler who was packing for a trip. When his friend came to pick him up the traveler had only a small suitcase.

"I'll be ready in a moment," he told his friend. "I just need to pack my guidebook, my compass, my sword and shield, a collection of poetry, my lamp, microscope, telescope, mirror, some biographies, my prayer book, some songs, sixty-six books that I've been reading, and my food."

The friend looked surprised. "How are you going to fit all that?"

"Not a problem," the Christian traveler replied, and put his Bible in the suitcase.

God has given us the equipment we need for the Christian's journey through life, but are we packing it? Or, are we leaving home without it?

After the death of Moses, God prepared Joshua to lead the Children of Israel on the last leg of their forty-year journey to the Promised Land. The Book of the Law —God's Word — was the only equipment they needed for their journey. God gave them instructions for every step they were to take. His Word was the guide to their daily activities, and the key to their success.

As it was with Joshua and the Children of Israel so it is with us today. To be fully equipped for our journey we must totally rely on and obey God's Word. We do not know where we are going. We cannot see the future. But, as the Psalmist says, "You guide me with your counsel, leading me to a glorious destiny." (Psalm 73:24 NLT).

To know in what direction God wants us to go — to know where He is leading us—we must read His Word daily and apply its teachings and principles to every aspect of our life. The Holy Bible — God's Positioning System—is our GPS. It's our all inclusive equipment for the journey. Don't leave home without it.

"Guide my steps by your Word, so I will not be overcome by evil." (Psalm 119:133 NLT).

– Rosetta Jamieson-Thomas

* * * *

Let the word of Christ dwell in you richly in all wisdom: teaching and admonishing one another in psalms and hymns and spiritual songs, singing with grace in your hearts to the Lord.

Colossians 3:16 KJV

Oh, how I love your instructions! I think about them all day long. Your commands make me wiser than my enemies, for they are my constant guide.

Psalm 119:97-98

Your word is a lamp to guide my feet and a light for my path. I've promised it once, and I'll promise it again: I will obey your righteous regulations.

Psalm 119:105-106

Exercise the Power

The Power of the Holy Spirit

But the Lord hardened Pharaoh's heart, so that he would not let the children of Israel go. And the Lord said unto Moses, Stretch out thine hand toward heaven, that there may be darkness over the land of Egypt, even darkness which may be felt. And Moses stretched forth his hand toward heaven; and there was a thick darkness in all the land of Egypt three days: They saw not one another, neither rose any from his place for three days: but all the children of Israel had light in their dwellings.

Exodus 10:20-2

"I declare war against sickness and diseases." That should be the Christians outcry. Sickness and diseases are not of God. He promises us abundant life and sickness is not a part of that. Am I saying that believers in God do not get sick? Not at all. Am I saying that diseases are always some judgment from God? Not at all.

"When I hear of cancer I get angry. I am thinking, "How dare the enemy afflict a child of God with this disease." When I hear of diabetes and all of those other debilitating diseases, I am equally angry. These diseases have been hanging around us far too long. God promises us that, "ye shall serve the LORD your God, and he shall bless thy bread, and thy water; and I will take sickness away from the midst of thee. There shall nothing cast their young, nor be barren, in thy land: the number of thy days I will fulfil."(Exodus 23:25-26) His promise to Israel extends to us today, the children of adoption. So if we are serving the Lord, why should we not expect that God will take away sickness from us?

Now there is some sickness that is unto death, and there is some sickness that is for the glory of God. Take a look at Job. He had a direct attack from the enemy. Although his friends would have liked him to believe that the horrible sequence of events was punishment from God, we know that was not the case. Sometimes we just have to wait for the manifestation of His glory. God rewarded Job "double for the trouble". In another situation, David prayed for the healing

37

of his son but because of God's judgment for David's actions, his son died. In the story of Lazarus, the account is that "When Jesus heard that, he said, This sickness is not unto death, but for the glory of God, that the Son of God might be glorified thereby." (John 11:4). We can also petition God to adjust the course. Isaiah 38 tells Hezekiah's story where, having been sick unto death, he lives to say, "The living, the living, he shall praise thee, as I do this day... The LORD was ready to save me..." We can seek the face of God for healing and, if it is His will, he will grant it to us.

God has declared to us that "If ye have faith as a grain of mustard seed, ye shall say unto this mountain, Remove hence to yonder place; and it shall remove; and nothing shall be impossible unto you. Howbeit this kind goeth not out but by prayer and fasting." Sometimes we just need to take it up a notch. Sometimes when you are seeking the face of the Lord and it seems like you are not breaking through, gather the saints. Our Heavenly Father is compassionate. "He will not always chide: neither will He keep his anger for ever. He hath not dealt with us after our sins; nor rewarded us according to our iniquities. For as the heaven is high above the earth, so great is his mercy toward them that fear him." Psalm 103:9-11 Abraham communed with God for his extended family. "Peradventure ten shall be found there..." and God said, "I will not destroy it for ten's sake". (Genesis 18:32)

"But as many as received him, to them gave he power to become the sons of God, even to them that believe on his name: Luke 11:12 "Then he called his twelve disciples together, and gave them power and authority over all devils, and to cure diseases. And he sent them to preach the kingdom of God, and to heal the sick." Luke 9:1-2 Sickness may come. As a matter of fact, if you are serving the Almighty God, you can guarantee that the enemy is on your trail. Most times, act as if he is not there, but still be very much aware of his antics. He is almost like a spoiled child seeking attention but far more dangerous. Be ready to resist the enemy so that he will flee from you. Exercise the power, call in reinforcement, abandon all else to seek the face of God for the divine presence of the Holy Spirit.

He promised us that, "When the enemy shall come in like a flood, the Spirit of the LORD shall lift up a standard against him." (Isaiah 59:19b)

Ruth Skerritt-Abraham

Build Loving Relationships

Ruth 1:16-17; 1 John 4:7-12, 21 (NKJV)

Beloved, let us love one another, for love is of God; and everyone who loves is born of God and loves God.

He who does not love does not know God, for God is love.

In this the love of God was manifested toward us, that God has sent His only begotten Son into the world, that we might live through Him.

In this is love, not that we loved God, but that He loved us and sent His Son to be the propitiation for our sins.

Beloved, if God so loved us, we also ought to love one another.

And this commandment we have from Him: that he who loves God must love his brother also.

Prayer Focus

Let your love for God show itself in your relationship with others.

Where You Lead I Will Follow

Love is defined as a strong emotion, causing one to appreciate, to take delight in, to have an excitement for, a burning desire, to crave the presence of.

LOVE.

Father, I love You. I appreciate You, I take my delight in You. When I consider that I am on Your mind, and in Your thoughts. That You consider me, evokes an excitement in my soul, that love gives way to my desire, yea longing to be in Your Presence.

My soul thirsteth for Thee.(Psalm 63:1)

LOVE

Love that created. Love that put on flesh. Love that hung on the cross. Love which pronounced Paradise to a thief, which died, resurrected, and ascended. Love that transforms, that saves. That never lacks power.

LOVE.

Father, lead me to love. My soul says yes! To love as love intensifies. Lead me. To be raptured, consumed, caught up as it absorbs me. Lead me, Father, to love, and I will follow.

Barbara D. Turner

Learn to Love the Lord

Read Psalm 119

Thy words have I hid in my heart that I might not sin against thee.

—Psalm 119:11

Psalm 119 may look very long and you may not want to read it, but you should. I read all 176 verses with my mother and I want to write something about it. Here is what I want to write: The Lord is good. If He is good to me, which He is, and He is good to you. How I love Him! I don't know about you. Do you love Him?

> *Blessed are the undefiled in the way,*
> *Who walk in the law of the Lord.*
> *Blessed are they that keep His testimonies*
> *And that seek Him with the whole heart.*
> *They also do no iniquities; they walk in his ways.*
> *Thou hast commanded us to keep thy precepts diligently.*
> *O that my ways were directed to keep Thy statues.*

(Psalm 119: 1-5)

So if I was to write one thing about what is in the Bible I would want people to love the Lord as much as I do. Do you love Him?

Dear Lord, I pray to you today that I would learn to love you in every way.

—**Annie Alexis Carty** *(8 years old)*

Built By Jesus

Read Ephesians 5:22 – 29

Unless the Lord builds the house, they labor in vain who build it

-Psalm 127:1 NKJV

Can a marriage last without Jesus as the glue? We don't think so. God the Father, the Son, and the Holy Spirit embodies all the ingredients for an enduring happy marriage.

God is love. (1 John. 4:8, 16) Love never fails. Our human definition of love, in love, and infatuation is something we can fall out of, or grow out of, but not God's. We have heard it repeatedly: "I don't love you anymore." "I fell in love and I fell out of love." "We grew apart, so we don't feel like we love each other anymore."

In Jesus Christ there is a definition of love that is so perfect and permanent that it endures into eternity. God loves us so much that He sent us Jesus: God in the human form who walked among us and died for us to show us how much we should love each other. Jesus said: "A new commandment I give to you, that you love one another; as I have loved you, that you also love one another." (John 13:34) God tell us, "And now abide faith, hope, love, these three; but the greatest of these is love." (1 Corinthians 13:13)

On marriage, God is specific. He says, "Wives, submit to your own husbands, as to the Lord. For the husband is the head of the wife, as also Christ is head of the church; and He is the Savior of the body." (Ephesians 5:22-23) God also says, "Husbands, love your wives just as Christ also loved the church and gave Himself for her… So husbands ought to love their wives as their own bodies; he who loves his wife loves himself. For no one ever hated his own flesh, but nourishes and cherishes it, just as the Lord does the church." (Ephesians 5:25, 28-29)

God is love. Father, please help us to love one another as you have loved us.

- Ricardo and Shauna Carty

The Act of Love

John 15: 1-14

Greater love has no man than this, that a man should lay down his life for his friends. Ye are my friends, if ye do whatsoever I command you.

John 15: 13-14

I am a big advocate for the popular phrase: "action speaks louder than words". We should always be mindful of the relationship between the words "love" and "action" before we nonchalantly whisper "I love you" to a loved one, or declare our love for our Lord. Love is an action word. So I thought that I should search to find out what the Bible says in support of this popular phrase.

I first stopped at John 3:16, "For God so loved the world that he gave his only begotten Son, that whosoever believeth in him should not perish but have everlasting life". God loves us. Therefore, he acted upon it and gave his life for our sins. I then read through the story where Peter denied Jesus but later, as if to give the disciple an opportunity to make amends and be reconciled, Jesus asked him, "Peter, do you love me?" He answered and Jesus said, "Feed my sheep". Three times altogether, in response to Peter's affirmative "Yes", Jesus responded with a command to do something.

All throughout the Bible are examples of the commission to act upon our love for God and for one another. One that stands out is the account where Jesus said, "If you love me, keep my commandments". John 14:15. This implies that we must submit in an act of obedience to show our love for our heavenly Father. I John 3:18 says, "My little children, let us not love in word, neither in tongue; but in deed and in truth." It's in the Word of God.

Lord God, help us to allow the love of Jesus to persuade us to do the will of our Heavenly Father.

-Ruth Skerritt-Abraham

Check Your Love

Read 1 Corinthians 13:4-8a

Above all things have fervent love for one another, for "love will cover a multitude of sins."

–I Peter 4:8 (NKJV)

Have you ever been so upset with a friend who did something that he/she knows you have a low tolerance for? For example, what if in the middle of a conversation, he/she belittles you by the words that he/she "harmlessly" uses? How do you respond? Do you snap back at him/her or do you calmly tell him/her later how he/she made you feel?

Check your love!

What if you are in a rush to get somewhere, and for whatever reason, you are running late? All of a sudden someone darts in front of you and cuts you off. You have nowhere to turn, so you slam on your brakes behind the person, nearly causing a traumatic accident. You resist the sudden desire to shout out "choice words" and make certain hand gestures.

Check your love!

How about if the person you are in love with has done something to hurt you, and it makes you jealous? He gallivants around being friendly with all of the ladies, just because he likes the attention. She maintains friendship with males that you are not comfortable with, just because they have been friends for a long time. How do you address him/her? Should you say something to your significant other or to the other parties involved?

Check your love!

Many people walk around wearing those popular wristbands labeled WWJD which stands for *What Would Jesus Do.* Jesus would do what is consistent with scriptures. Just like Jesus we should respond in the true meaning of love, as defined and outlined in 1 Corinthians 13: 4-8a which we have just read. Any response other than that will not be given out in love.

What has your response been in the situations that life has given you? Under what circumstances has your love been challenged?

In everything that you think say or do, remember to check your love!

– Marette A. Moore

Frankly Speaking

Read Ephesians 4: 15-25

Let your speech be always with grace, seasoned with salt, that ye may know how ye ought to answer every man.

–Colossians 4:6

Some people have the innate ability to speak their mind, shoot from the hip, and tell it as it is. But there are also straight shooters whose words are meant to hurt. They are cruel and cutting, and lack the grace that Scripture describes as "seasoning" for the tongue. It is commendable to get straight answers when seeking truth for life's difficult questions, but only when the words spoken will prove to be edifying to the hearers.

The definition of the word frank is "to be free in uttering real sentiments" but it's very dangerous not to think before one speaks, thus, proceeding to blurt out the first thing that comes to mind. It may all be truth, but it was certainly not tempered with love. Spiritual maturity in Christ warrants that we deal with each other as we would want to be dealt with ourselves.

James 1:19 states, "My brethren, let every man be swift to hear, slow to speak, and slow to wrath." In other words, keep your ears perked to listen, but also discipline yourself to put your lips on pause before parting them to utter words filled with graceless, tasteless remarks. Frankly speaking, Proverb 29:11 says it best: "A fool uttered all his mind but a wise man will keep it till afterwards." Lord, help me to think first, and gear up my mouth second — not vice versa.

You can be lovingly frank without being frankly mean.

- **Margaret Moore**

48

Angel

Be not forgetful to entertain strangers, for thereby some have entertained angels unawares.

Hebrews 13:2

From the foundation of the world
God thought on you
And in the same kyros moment
He thought on me

And . . . THE WORD became flesh and dwelt among us!

He breathed the breath of life into my spirit
And into your spirit
Made in His image and after HIS likeness
Kyros!!!

Tested . . . tried . . . testified . . . Kyros!!!

Before you knew my name
You knew . . . my worship, and I knew . . . yours
We knew . . . the pain.
Yet, the savor of the praise

To go from brokenness to breakthrough
From hemorrhaging to healing
From outcasts to over-comers
Kyros!!!

Stranger . . . Angel . . . Friend . . .

And THE WORD became flesh and dwelt among us.

- Barbara D. Turner

LORD, How Deep Is Your Love!

And now abideth faith, hope, and love, these three: but the greatest of these is love.

1 Corinthians 13:13

Lord, who could measure your love?
The height, the depth, the width . . . the breadth of your love.

When we enter your presence, we are endued with your power
You transformed the woman with the issue of blood
You transformed the man at the pool of Bethesda
You transformed Saul on the road to Damascus
And you have transformed us.

Because of your love you created us in your image, and after your likeness
You humbled yourself to death on the cross.
How deep is your love, Lord!

The depth of your love is like your blood
It never loses its power!

The width of your love abides
It opens the way to "the secret place" where we can experience
Your grace and mercy

The height of your love gives us strength, courage, and power.
You are our joy.

The breadth of your love is everlasting
Your love rests upon us, and gives us new life
Gift-wrapped, rich in birthright and inheritance
How deep is your love, Lord!

We are forgiven, accepted in the beloved, because you first loved us.

You assigned your love to work on our behalf, while we were yet sinners.

And that love isn't finished with us.

For that love, we call You, Savior, Master, King . . . Friend!

-CLIMB Ministry

Love & Forgiveness

Bear with each other and forgive whatever grievances you may have against one another. Forgive as the Lord forgave you.

Colossians 3:13 (NIV)

Not too long ago, I was upset with one of my sisters, and felt that I was right. I was the oldest, and it seemed like we just couldn't see eye to eye on some issues. For a long time pride caused little, or no communication between us. I prayed frequently about the matter, but I felt that my prayers were not heard. As time moved on, I began to feel like a hypocrite, and rightfully so. We are hypocrites if we claim to love God and have bitterness and resentment in our hearts. Just like Hannah, I cried out to God sincerely, "Lord, I want my sister back. Help me to forgive her and forgive me for my un-forgiveness".

I say to you if you are holding on to hurt feelings, get over them. Be the first to forgive. It doesn't matter who is right or wrong. It may not be easy, but it is mandatory for us to love, and forgive one another. Forgiveness will bring victory in the healing of your body, soul, and mind.

I was the first to reach out to my sister. It was as if she was also waiting for the moment when we would reconcile. She was happy, and so was I. We couldn't stop telling each other how much we loved each other. I thank God for the renewed relationship that I have with my sister, and both of us know who made it possible.

Father God, give us the strength to resolve our daily issues. Create in us a clean heart, and a renewed spirit to sincerely follow your commandment to love others, so that we will not allow unresolved issues to cause un-forgiveness in our heart. In Jesus name I pray. Amen.

Don't let unresolved issues hinder you, and don't let anything or anyone block your way to the kingdom.

-Vicie Carter

Be Available For His Service

Read 1 Samuel 3:1-10; Isaiah 6:8

And the Lord called Samuel again the third time. So he arose and went to Eli and said, "Here am I, for you did call me." Then Eli perceived that the Lord had called the boy.

Therefore Eli said to Samuel, "Go, lie down; and it shall be, if He calls you, that you must say, "Speak, Lord, for your servant hears." So Samuel went and lay down in his place.

Now the Lord came and stood and called as at other times, "Samuel, Samuel!" And Samuel answered, "Speak, Lord, for your servant hears."
1 Samuel 3: 8-10 (NKJV)

Also I heard the voice of the Lord, saying:
"Whom shall I send,
And who will go for Us?"
Then I said, "Here am I, send me."
Isaiah 6:8 (NKJV)

Prayer Focus

Give thanks to "God who has saved us and called us with a holy calling, not according to our works, but according to His purpose . . ." (2 Timothy 1:9). Pray for an understanding of the purpose to which you have been called, for courage to move into whatever He has for you to do, knowing that whoever He calls He empowers.

How to Accept a Miracle

Read Luke 1

Then Mary said, "Behold the maidservant of the Lord! Let it be to me according to your word…"

–Luke 1:38(NKJV

Have you ever been confronted by the promise that God will do something impossible for you? How did you react? We can learn from Mary how to receive a miracle. Mary was a virgin girl when an angel appeared to her with an impossible declaration. Then the angel said to her, "Do not be afraid, Mary, for you have found favor with God. And behold, you will conceive in your womb and bring forth a Son, and shall call His name Jesus. He will be great, and will be called the Son of the Highest; and the Lord God will give Him the throne of His father David. And He will reign over the house of Jacob forever, and of His kingdom there will be no end." (Luke 1:30-33)

The angel promised Mary that God would use her to give birth to our Lord and Savior Jesus Christ. Mary didn't say she didn't believe it. She didn't argue that it couldn't happen. She didn't say she hadn't prayed for this, or she didn't want it to happen. **Instead, she asked, how**. Mary didn't complain that she couldn't handle the responsibility. She didn't express concern over what other people would think. She didn't point out that it would cramp her lifestyle. **She accepted**. Then Mary said, "Behold the maidservant of the Lord! Let it be to me according to your word…" (Luke 1:38)

Later, she got together with Elizabeth **and praised the Lord**— even before the miracle of Jesus' birth occurred. And Mary said, "My soul magnifies the Lord, and my spirit has rejoiced in God my Savior…" (Luke 1:46-55)

Mary had faith in God and believed the angel who had assured her: "For with God nothing will be impossible."

Father, please help us to find your possibility in impossible situations.

- Ricardo and Shauna Carty

Heed Now or Pay Later

Read Jonah 1:1-16

"Arise, go to Nineveh, that great city, and cry against it; for their wickedness is come up before me."

-Jonah1:1 NKJV

There are times in our lives when God will tell us to go somewhere and/or do something that we don't understand. It is in these times that our faith and trust in God is displayed. Our level of obedience will be made obvious by our reaction and response to His orders. Jonah responded incorrectly. He ignored God and His instructions and decided to create his own itinerary. As a result, Jonah placed many people in the path of danger. He endangered the crew of the ship on its journey to Tarshish. He endangered the people of Nineveh by delaying the message sent for them from God. Jonah even placed himself in a precarious situation in which he had to endure three days and three nights in the belly of a whale.

Two chapters after Jonah's initial disobedience, God reiterated His original directions: "Arise, go unto Nineveh, that great city, and preach unto it the preaching that I bid thee." Jonah 3:2. As Christians, we must realize that our disobedience does not only bring pain and anguish to us individually, but also to our family, friends and those we come in contact with. Our ill-advised decisions may also delay the delivery of a warning from God. In the end, after all the pain, problems, and trouble we've caused, we will still have to obey God, just like Jonah.

Father God, please teach me to be obedient to your directions so that your will for my life may be fulfilled. Search my heart, Lord: remove anything that would cause me to hesitate in allowing you to lead me down the paths you have tread for my life. Lord, create in me a clean, obedient heart so that your purpose for the directions you give me will become my goal. In the mighty name of Jesus I pray. Amen.

You can't run from God.

- **Michael W. Tyree**

The Supper

Luke 14: 16-24

But seek ye first the kingdom of God and his righteousness and all these things shall be added unto you.

-Matthew 6:33

It was a great supper. There were special invitees. Some of the preferred guests were influential men of substance, and most likely, well connected. Others were perhaps in the process of establishing themselves in life. To cater for such guests the cuisine was excellent; the décor was elegant; the atmosphere was lovely, and servants were at their best. But when the servants went out to inform the special guests that supper was ready, these guests all had vain excuses and declined the invitation to this great supper.

The master of the house became angry. His preparations were grand, but his preferred guests were no-shows. In his anger, it seemed it no longer mattered who came to the supper. His preparations must not be wasted so he quickly sent his servants to extend the invitation to everyone. "Go out into the highways and hedges, and compel *them* to come in, that my house may be filled."(Luke 14:23)

These invitees were appreciative of the invitation because they all had limitations. Unlike the first group, they were disabled in one form or other and welcomed the ambiance and the supper offered by the master. The first group, in their abundance or with the excitement of promising prospects, saw no benefit in attending the supper.

The Lord invites you to take time to have supper with him. His supper begins with surrendering your life to him, acknowledging him as Lord, continuing in prayer, and reading his word. He gives us direction for living as "His word is a lamp unto our feet and a light to our path." He is our shepherd and we shall not want. There will always be food at his table.

Blessed is he that shall eat bread in the kingdom of God. (Luke14:15)

-Yonette Morrison

Where Is the Passion?

Read Acts 1: 1-14

"I am the way, the truth and the life, no man cometh unto the Father, but by me."

–John 14:6

I was on the PATH train this morning and there was a gentleman who witnessed about Jesus from the beginning of the train ride at Newark until we got to the World Trade Center. He kept talking about the promises of Jesus and that he loved us so much that he gave his only Son so that we might have a way of escape. He even invited the audience to pray the sinner's prayer, by faith, believing that if you confess with your mouth and believe in your heart that Jesus is Lord, He is faithful and just to forgive you and to cleanse you from all of your unrighteousness. He had a passion for Christ; he was mindful of his obligation to preach the gospel. He was not ashamed. The Spirit of the Lord is upon him and this man continued to witness on his walk to his workplace. I admired his boldness . . . . and then I was convicted.

I thought. How am I fulfilling my obligation? Where is my passion? Was I hiding my light under a bushel? This brought me back to the account of John the Baptist, "the voice of one crying in the wilderness" telling everyone to "prepare ye the way of the Lord, make his paths straight" (Mark 1:3). That wilderness exists just the same today. It's the same density, different trees. If we observe the world today there seems to be no set path for right or wrong. We just tolerate everything.

As witnesses for Christ, you and I are commissioned to preach the gospel so that the path is clearly seen. The Spirit of truth lives within us even more so than John the Baptist. We need to allow him to guide us into all truth so that we may be witnesses and glorify God.

Lord, give us boldness today to show our love and passion for Christ and for mankind, that we may use every fiber in our being to fulfill our commission.

- Ruth Skerritt-Abraham

Unproven Armor

Read 1 Samuel 17: 38-40

Give diligence to make your calling and election sure: for if ye do these things, ye shall never fall.

-2 Peter 1:10

King Saul chose specific armor for David to wear before confronting the giant Goliath. David obliged the king, but once dressed, he realized that the metal coat and brass helmet could impede his victory over the enemy because he had not tested the battle gear.

David said to Saul, "I cannot go with these, for I have not proven them." And David put them off.

Sometimes we enter into battle tripping, falling, and weighted down because we're wearing someone else's gears. Perhaps we're donning someone else's ministry gift and have not diligently proven what God has specifically chosen for us.

What David did was wise. He took off what wasn't designed for him, realizing that what may be a perfect fit for one may be ill-fitted for another, and could result in disaster. So he faced the giant wearing his own armor and God gave him the victory.

Lord, help me to walk in my anointing, being sure of my gifts and calling. Amen

-Margaret Moore

By Way of A Detour

Read Deuteronomy 30:1-3

For I know what plans I have for you, declares the Lord; plans to prosper you and not to harm you; plans to give you a hope and a future.

–Jeremiah 29:11

When we submit our life to Jesus there is a longing that finally gets satisfied. However, when the testing comes, as he demands of us to take a step of faith to do his will and walk into his purpose, we begin to waiver and are fearful that we are not up to the task.

Do we know that who the Lord calls he equips? In our state of wavering, we run, we hide; we throw a pity party and come up with all sorts of reasons why we are not on board with God's plan. The children of Israel took a detour on their way to the land of "milk and honey". For that reason, Moses got fed up and as a result forfeited his entry into the Promised Land. Jonah fled to Joppa via Tarshish instead of going to Nineveh as the Lord commanded. Elijah threw a pity party when he was running for his life from Jezebel.

As we find ourselves wandering in our wilderness or in the belly of a "whale" of a situation, the good news is that there is restoration. The children of Israel made it into the Promised Land. Jonah landed in Nineveh as was intended, and the people received their deliverance. Even though Elijah was gripped by moments of fear after so boldly expressing his faith in God and slaying all the prophets of Baal, God put him back on track and encouraged him to get himself together.

Just as God did with Israel, Jonah, and Elijah, He is saying to us that there's work to be done. Get back in the will of God. "In whom also we have obtained an inheritance, being predestinated according to the purpose of him who worketh all things after the counsel of his own will. (Ephesians 1:11)

Dear Lord, we pray that your perfect will be done in our lives.

-Ruth Skerritt-Abraham

Order, in the Courtroom!

Read Psalm 75

"Lift not up your horn on high: speak not with a stiff neck. For promotion cometh neither from the east, nor from the west, nor from the south. But God is the judge: he putteth down one, and setteth up another.

–Psalm 75:5-7.

I wonder how many times we need to be reminded that promotion comes from the Lord. There is really nothing that we can do on our own, or are so capable of accomplishing without God. For King Uzziah, the fame and fortune got to his head so much that he figured that he could exalt himself above God's appointed and do the job of the Priests. Do you know that there are consequences for acting out of your place?

Roles were established with the children of Israel since they were in the wilderness. Moses had his role, the elders had their role and the Priests had their role. It's called order. We cannot be busy dipping in everything, you'll get worn out. We serve a God who is very practical but the "big head" would do you in. And that's what happened to King Uzziah. He was immediately afflicted with a disease – leprosy.

Let's be careful not to trespass outside of the boundaries of the task that God has appointed unto us. The job of the Pastor must be done by the Pastor; the job of the Deacon must be done by the Deacon. I dare the Deacon to try to get up in the pulpit to give instructions to the flock. With God there is order. There are no limits with God, but there is order.

Help us, O Lord, to seek your face and understand the parameters of the task that you have assigned us. When we can do nothing within these parameters to remedy a situation, let us pray for the solution. Amen

- Ruth Skerritt-Abraham

Are We Serving God or Man?

Read Colossians 3:23

"No one can serve two masters for either he will hate the one, and love the other, or else he will be loyal to the one and despise the other. You cannot serve God and mammon."

—Matthew 6: 24 NKJV

I believe this scripture is meant in every sense of the word. Now this is my understanding. That's why we pray for wisdom every time we read His word.

As Christians we become members of a church where we are usually assigned to a ministry according to our gifts, to glorify God. Romans 12: 6-7: Having then gifts differing according to the grace that is given to us; let us use them: If prophecy, let us prophesy in proportion to our faith; or ministry, let us use it in our ministering; he who teaches, in teaching.

But when someone criticizes or just disagrees with us, we become discouraged and stop our ministering. This happens not just in the church, at home, the work place; wherever we are giving God the glory.

Colossians 3:23: And whatever you do, do it heartily, as to the Lord and not to men. Remember the devil's main purpose is to kill, steal and destroy (John 10:10). Let's not forget we serve a God that will never leave us or forsake us, and will fight our battles. Trials and tribulations will come that's for sure. So let us keep "rejoicing in hope; patient in tribulation; continuing steadfastly in prayer." (Romans 12:12)

Dear Father, please help us to cheerfully do your will.

Serve God in all that you do.

—Ricardo and Shauna Carty

What's In Your Hands?

Read Exodus 4:1-5

And the Lord said unto him (Moses), "What is that in thine hand?"

- Exod.4:2 KJV

Capital One Credit Card Company has a television commercial which has aired hundreds of times by now. In this commercial, scores of Vikings are invading, and are just about to overtake all of your properties, possessions, and persons. Just before they come in to take your life you open your wallet, and in the nick of time, you pull out your Capital One Credit Card . . . . They see your credit card, back off, totally give up chasing you, and go after somebody else who doesn't have a Capital One Credit Card. The representative for Capital One concludes the commercial by asking you a poignant question: "What's in your wallet?"

We now rewind our thoughts back several millennia to a time when God appeared to a lowly shepherd named Moses, who witnessed a bush on fire. Amazingly, the burning bush was not being burnt by the flames. We might say that this is where Moses experienced an epiphany with God. God, in this attention-getting demonstration, used Moses' curiosity to draw him into God's divine purpose for his life's ministry.

God was mostly concerned about Moses' availability for ministry, not his ability to produce impressive curriculum vitae, or to demonstrate the mastery of articulating perfect Hebrew idiom. God wasn't concerned about Moses possessing superhuman or supernatural powers in order for him to be His ambassador of righteousness. God simply wanted Moses to answer the call to ministry, but more importantly, it was time for Moses to "use (The Rod) that was in his hands."

No excuses are adequate responses to reject God's call especially when we come to the realization that "it is He that made us, and not we ourselves." God knows our limitations and our capabilities.

After all, He is our designer, manufacturer, service and maintenance provider. So what's your excuse? "What's In Your Hands?"

Lord Jesus, I surrender my mind, body, and soul to you. Use me however you see fit, that you might receive the honor, glory and praise, through the life that I live, and the service that I give.

- **James E. Moore, Sr.**

The Peace of God
- *Reflections on Retirement*

Read Philippians 4: 6-8

The peace of God which surpasses all understanding will guard your hearts and minds through Christ Jesus.

Philippians 4:7 NKJV

Now that I am retired I wonder what's next after thirty years of working at the same job; getting up early to travel to the same location all those years. Those years were a blessing from God. Now, even though I worry at times, God's peace keeps me hopeful because I know He has a plan for me. I just don't know yet what it is but as long as I stay true to Him, I'll find the answer in the Bible.

The apostle Paul advises us to turn our worries into prayers. If you want to worry less, pray more. Through prayer I realize that God gives us peace of mind through Christ. God wants us to recognize how good He has been to us these years. He enables us to move to the next plan that He has for our lives. All we have to do is continue to trust Him, obey Him, pray and wait on Him to take us to higher levels of fulfillment in Him.

Thank you, God, for the years I spent on my previous job. Thank you for allowing me more opportunities to serve you better. Thank you for the peace I have in knowing that my steps are ordered by you.

Whatever God has for us to do after we retire, we must remember that we never retire from doing the work of the Lord.

- Alexis Hardy

Give Thanks

Read Luke 17::12 – 17

And one of them, when he saw that he was healed, returned, and with a loud voice glorified God, and fell on his face at His feet, giving Him thanks. And he was a Samaritan.
So Jesus answered and said, "Were there not ten cleanse; but where are the nine? Were there not any found who returned to give glory to God except this foreigner?"

Oh, give thanks to the Lord: for he is good! For His mercy endures forever.
Oh, give thanks to the God of gods! For his mercy endures forever.
Oh, give thanks to the Lord of lords! For his mercy endures forever.
Psalm 136:1- 3(NKJV)

Oh, give thanks unto the Lord! Call upon His name: make known His deeds among the people.
Sing to him; sing psalms to him: talk of all His wondrous works.
Glory in His holy name; let the hearts of those rejoice who seek the Lord!
Psalm105:1-3(NKJV)

Prayer Focus

In everything give thanks, for this is the will of God in Christ Jesus for you.

1 Thesalonians 5:18

Jesus to the Rescue

Read Psalm 91:14-16

The righteous cry and the Lord heareth and delivereth.

–Psalm 34:17

As a result of being wounded in warfare during World War II, my Dad became a recipient of the Purple Heart Medal of Honor.

Fragments from the explosion — a land mine — pierced his legs leaving him injured, bleeding and immobile. A fellow soldier came to his rescue.

Thank God, Dad wasn't left as a forgotten casualty; as Christians neither are we. Jesus said, "I will never leave thee or forsake thee." (Hebrew 13:5). When we have been sorely wounded during spiritual battles, it's the Lord who hears our cry, answers our call, and delivers us from trouble.

We take courage in knowing that He came all the way from heaven to earth to declare war on sin. And when we are hurt we have the promise that He will rescue us again and again,

God has a special ministry waiting for the recovered wounded. (II Corinthians 1:3). Lord, when I'm down help me to remember I'm not alone.

- Margaret Moore

How Valuable Is Your Gift?

Read 1 John 3:17-18

For everyone to whom much is given, from him much will be required.

-Luke12:48b, NKJV

Jesus Christ set the ultimate example of love when He gave His life for us. We, in turn, should show our love for one another through selfless, sacrificial acts of kindness.

When my youngest son was in college he taught me a very valuable lesson in giving. I had just come home from work and was busily trying to get through some household chores when my phone rang.

"Mom, I didn't have enough money to pay the toll on the turnpike so I got onto a local street. Now I don't know how to get home from here."

I didn't know the neighborhood well enough to give him specific directions but I had a vague idea of how to get to him. So I went looking for him. Needless to say, I was very annoyed. He had left home with enough money for lunch, gas and tolls. How could he be so irresponsible? Didn't he know better than to spend his toll money on something else? Not only was he going to be late for his part-time job, he had also interrupted the flow of my day, and I didn't have time for that.

"Why did you spend your toll money?" I demanded impatiently the minute I found him. "Where's your sense of responsibility?"

"I bought food for a homeless man and gave him the change."

"And just how did you expect to get home from school when you gave away your last dollar?" I snapped.

He just looked at me, shrugged his shoulders and said, "That didn't matter."

Immediately I felt guilty and ashamed of my reaction. Instead of commending his selflessness I was yelling at him. He had given all he had without thinking of his personal needs.

Are we willing and ready to put the needs of others ahead of our own needs? It's not enough for us to say, "Thank You, Jesus, for all you've given me." We must also thank Him in a tangible way by sharing the gifts and resources He has blessed us with even when it means personal sacrifice.

Jesus gave His life for us. That's priceless! How valuable is your gift to others?

– Rosetta Jamieson-Thomas

Give Thanks

Read Psalm 107

Oh, that men would give thanks to the Lord for His goodness, and for His wonderful works to the children of men.

-Psalm 107:8 NKJV

At Thanksgiving, we invite family and friends over and have a big feast, forgetting that if it were not for God's mercy, it would not be possible. Romans 1:21—because, although they knew God, they did not glorify Him as God, nor were thankful, but became futile in their thoughts...

Every morning that Shauna and I get up, one of the ways we give thanks is by reciting Psalms 118:24—This is the day the Lord has made; we will rejoice and be glad in it. Every day on my way to work I would see the homeless people on the street corners asking for a handout; that's when I realized that could be me. Psalm 107:1--Oh give thanks unto the Lord, for He is good: for His mercy endures forever.

At Christmas, we shop until we drop, yet most of the gifts are returned or better yet put in a closet to collect dust. If someone less fortunate asks for a helping hand we look the other way. Deuteronomy 15:11—For the poor shall never cease out of the land: therefore I command thee, saying, Thou shalt open thine hand wide unto thy brother, to thy poor, and to the needy, in the land. Yes! Even our enemies. Romans 12:2—Therefore if thine enemy hunger, feed him; if he thirst, give him drink: for in so doing thou shalt heap coals of fire on his head.

Personally, I don't think my family and I can thank God enough for all He has done for us.

Father, please help us to give You thanks and praise, regardless of our circumstances.

- Ricardo and Shauna Carty

71

No Leftovers, Please!

Read Leviticus 23: 9-14

Honor the Lord with thy substance and with the first fruits of all thy increase.

-Proverb 3:9 NKJV

The church in which I worshipped in the Caribbean celebrated an annual Harvest of Thanksgiving. This was a day on which everyone gave the best of whatever they produced as a gift to the church. The Harvest of Thanksgiving was a very festive occasion, much like a country fair, and everyone in the neighborhood looked forward to this day. After the items were blessed they were sold and the money raised was given to the church.

This community of believers gave the best of their produce as a reminder that all that we are and all that we have belong to the Lord – our life, time, talents, money – everything. When the Children of Israel harvested their new crops they were required by the Law to first present God's portion to Him before they could eat any of it. Likewise, we honor our Lord and Savior Jesus Christ and demonstrate our gratitude for what He has done for us by giving back to Him the first portion of what He has blessed us with.

Father God, in the name of Jesus, I thank and praise You for making me who I am and for blessing me abundantly. Teach me the meaning of sacrificial giving and give me the courage to put you first in all areas of my life. "Take my life and let it be consecrated, Lord to thee. Take my moments and my days. Let them flow in constant praise."

The essence of worship is honoring Jesus for who He is and giving back to Him that which is most valuable.

-Rosetta Jamieson-Thomas

The Giver of Life

Read Acts 17:24-28

Let everything that hath breath praise the Lord. Praise ye the Lord.

–Psalm 150:6

After a good night's sleep, I awoke one morning but could not breathe without restraint. My first breath upon opening my eyes was accompanied by sharp pains in my chest. For the next 60 seconds of eternity, I could only pant shallow breaths – afraid to breathe freely lest the pain hasten some unfortunate occurrence whereby I could not partake of God's life-sustaining air…

That morning was another turning point in my life. Hence, upon taking my first breath of air daily, I realize just how precious life really is and I'm happy to proclaim "Hallelujah! Thank you, Jesus, for this day."

God has many ways of shaping hearts of gratitude, and in appreciation of life, we eventually come to understand that we must no longer take our lives for granted but should have joy in praising Him who woke us up this morning. Our heavenly father knows what we need better than we do, for He created us.

Good morning, Father God, thank you for waking me up to see another day; you didn't have to do it, but you did. Help me to praise you as long as you give me life.

– Deborah Hardy

Thoughts of Gratitude

Read Psalm 34:1-22

I will bless the Lord at all times: his praise shall continually be in my mouth.

Psalm 34:1

When I think of the goodness of Jesus and all that he has done for me, I remain thankful to God for the mercies that He extends towards me each day of my life. I am always inspired by one of my favorite passages of scripture – Psalm 34. Truly, I will bless the Lord at all times and His praise shall continually be in my mouth.

On October 2nd, my mother celebrated her 85th birthday. It was so exciting for me to be able to share cake and celebrate with her on this side of Jordan. Life throws us a lot of trials and tribulations and I guarantee you that my mother has been dealt a few. However, through it all, God remains faithful. We are reminded in the book of Lamentations 3: 21-23, "This I recall to my mind, therefore have I hope. It is of the Lord's mercies that we are not consumed, because his compassions fail not. They are new every morning: great is thy faithfulness."

I am grateful for all that God has done; the victories that have already been won. My soul shall forever boast in the Lord. Those of you who honor and adore Him, I encourage you to magnify the Lord with me, and let us exalt His name. For those who need to get to know him, I ask that you taste and see that the Lord is good.

Innumerable blessings await you if you only trust in Him.

-Billy McDowell

The Ultimate Family Reunion

I know both how to be abased and I know how to abound everywhere and in all things I am instructed both to be full and to be hungry, both to abound and to suffer need. I can do all things through Christ which strengtheneth me.

Philippians 4:12-13

My brethren, count it all joy when ye fall into divers temptations; knowing this, that the trying of our faith worketh patience.

James 1:2-3

A family reunion is a celebration of uniting with families that represent our heritage, a sharing time and conversation that links others to our past as well as to our future. I ask that you reflect for a moment. Think about the loved ones who have passed on to Glory—parents, children, relatives, even close friends. Imagine the struggles they may have had or may have suffered through, so that you also could overcome obstacles and make it through your struggles today. While remembering loved ones gone on to Glory before us may be difficult to understand, painful to remember, and sorrowful to think of, reflect joyfully on how those loved ones endured their life to receive everlasting victory in Jesus! Now, think in the present... count your blessings for still having other loved ones in this present life...parents, children, relatives, and close friends.

Whether or not you are thinking of loved ones who have passed on or thinking of loved ones still with you in this life, my hope is that we would all take time to reflect on the victories we have had in life. Know that each victory we achieve is because of those loved ones who have made it possible for us through their own struggles and subsequent victories. Think of how your life's victories might help bring victory to someone else in your lineage after you have gone on to Glory!

As for me, before thanking my parents who are still alive and well as of this writing, and before thanking my husband for marrying me into another loving, Christian family of abundant proportion, prior to giving thanks for our children, my sister, my cousins, dear friends, their families and friends…and on it goes. Before thanking God for them all, and above all, I am thankful for the One whose heritage is greater and above all histories of this world. His is The One whose history and heritage has been gifted to us because of His love for us! HIS STORY, the history of JESUS, His life, His death on the Cross and His resurrection, and ultimately, His Reunion with THE FATHER!

Be confident that, if we believe, confess and receive it, our greatest reunions, thankfully, will not be those here on earth, but our greatest reunion will be that of Everlasting Life with our Lord and Savior Jesus Christ! Therefore, count it ALL joy! Think victoriously, and realize that with God, we can rise above every obstruction of justice; we can rise above every failure, every fear, every fault, and every foe. Our ultimate victory comes because His Story led the way. Our heritage in Jesus makes it possible for us to overcome thoughts of both past and ever-present struggles, and causes us to rise up and pursue victories for the future! Because of God's Ultimate Sacrifice of His Son, we will have the Ultimate Family Reunion with God the Father!

Evonne Tyree

Stay Connected

Daniel 6:10, Psalm 91:1-2; 62:5 (NKJV)

Now when Daniel knew that the writing was signed, he went home; And in the upper room, with his windows open towards Jerusalem, he knelt down on his knees three times that day, and prayed, and gave thanks before his God, as was His custom since early days.

Daniel 6:10

He who dwells in the secret place of the Most High
Shall abide under the Shadow of the Almighty
I will say of the Lord, "He is my refuge and my fortress;
My God, in Him I will trust."

Psalm 91:1-2

Prayer Focus

My soul, waits silently for God alone,
For my expectation is from Him

Psalm 62:5

An Established Mind

Read Isaiah 26:3-4

Commit thy works unto the Lord and thy thoughts shall be established.

–Proverb 16:3

Each and every day the good Lord raises us from our night-time slumber gives us another opportunity to embark upon some type of meaningful work assignment. Jesus told His disciples in St. John 9:4, "I must work the works of Him that sent me while it is day: the night cometh when no man can work."

When we commit our daily tasks to the Lord asking that He takes them unto Himself, that commitment opens the door for Him to step into our thoughts and begin to speak direction to our minds.

The ideal way to start the day is in seeking His guidance. But if during the day because of our busyness we find ourselves avalanched with responsibilities and the work-loads leads us to experience mixed-up emotions, confused thinking or even uncertain directions . . . stop! Cease what you're doing. Mentally pause, and whisper a prayer to commit your undertakings to the Lord. After a deep breath, you can watch how He works to settle your thoughts and strengthen your resolve.

Not only does Jesus want to order our steps He delights in establishing our thoughts. God alone can speak calm to confusion.

In a society of frazzled nerves and discombobulate thinking, Lord remind me to always look up to you.

- Margaret Moore

Return to Jesus

Read Luke 22:31-62

"For whoever is ashamed of Me and My words in this adulterous and sinful generation, of him the Son of Man will also be ashamed when He comes in the glory of His Father with the holy angels."

-Mark 8:38 NKJV

The apostle Simon Peter walked with Jesus in the flesh. He witnessed Jesus at work on earth. Yet, when the matter was called into question, Peter denied knowing Jesus three times (Luke 22:55-62)

This lapse in faith that happened to Peter happens to us regularly. Born again Christians turn into unbelievers. I waver each time I know my faith is alienating me from someone I love. Yet, I know I'm right about Jesus and my stand for Him must be public and it must be sincere.

"For whoever is ashamed of Me and My words in this adulterous and sinful generation, of him the Son of Man will also be ashamed when He comes in glory of His Father with the holy angels." (Mark 8:38)

But Peter did not stay down. He rose again as a mighty witness for the kingdom of God, testifying of Jesus and, by faith, carrying on great works. Simon Peter reconciled with Jesus declaring his love three times: "Simon, son of Jonah, do you love Me? And he said to Him, 'Lord, You know all things; You know that I love You." (John 21:15-17)

Have you strayed from a close relationship with the Lord Jesus? Maybe it's time you came back.

Father, please draw me closer to You and help me to never be ashamed of You.

- Ricardo and Shauna Carty

Got Bars? In a Dead Zone?

Read Deuteronomy 28: 1-2

The words that I speak unto you, they are spirit and they are life.

-John 6: 63b

"Can you hear me now?" Ever get on your cell phone in your car, at home, or somewhere noisy, and not being able to hear the person at the other end? It is difficult to hear through all of the distractions and surrounding noise. Even more frustrating is the attempt to have a conversation with someone on a cell phone with little or no bars, or worse, in a dead zone. If the reception doesn't improve and either of these situations persists for more than a few seconds one usually ends up with a dropped call.

Well with God it's not different. When we are talking to God we need to have areas free of distractions and the noise of life. If we are in a spiritual dead zone we could be causing our connections with Christ to drop. When we frequent the dead zone our spiritual bars are not up to receive God's call to our Spirit so we miss out on what He is saying. God wants to say so much to us but we have to get to a place where there is reception.

Where do we go when we need spiritual reception? *The House of God? The Word of God? The Presence of God?* Pick one. Got Bars? We must step out of the dead zone and take some time to get away from the noise and distraction of life and step into the spiritual reception of abundant life. Get into the "hearing zone". There are rewards for listening. "And it shall come to pass, if thou shalt hearken diligently unto the voice of the LORD thy God, to observe and to do all His commandments which I command thee this day, that the LORD thy God will set thee on high above all nations of the earth."

Speak Lord, I am listening. I will be still and know that you are God.

-James Moore, Jr.

Kingdom Seekers

Read Matthew 6:25-34

But seek ye first the kingdom of God and His righteousness; and all these things shall be added unto you.

–Matthew 6:33

Are you a Kingdom Seeker? A Righteous Wannabe? Kingdom seekers and "righteous wannabes" don't worry about necessities because they know God will supply their every need. The Word of God, as stated in Matthew 6:33, proves this. But what are the things to which this verse refers?

Matthew 6: 25 and 31 describe these things as what we will eat, what we will drink, and even what clothing we will put on! These are the things that are identified as what the Gentiles or unsaved worry about. In these challenging times, with so many things demanding our attention, it is so easy to focus on things – our earthly possessions and our material needs— and give them, and not God, first priority.

When we seek things at the expense of our personal relationship with God we lose out on God's blessings. But as long as we seek the Kingdom of God and His righteousness first, all these things that the world always worries about will be added unto us. God has promised to supply all our needs and He will when we trust him and put Him above all else in our life. As heirs of God and joint-heirs with Christ all our needs are met through Him who loves us and gave His life for us. So don't worry; depend on God.

Lord, we thank you that you have provided all things for us. Help us to be true kingdom seekers; to put our trust in you, and our relationship with you above all else.

- James Moore, Jr.

Eyes, Ears and Expectancy

Eyes have not seen, ears have not heard and neither has entered into the heart of man, the things which God hath prepared for them that love him.

I Corinthians 2:9

Head . . . shoulders, knees and toes, knees and toes
Head . . . shoulders, knees and toes, knees and toes
Eyes and ears . . . mouth and nose.
Head . . . shoulders, knees and toes, knees and toes

Any of you who have children or have worked around children know this song, and probably are singing the melody as you read the words. My son loves this song, especially when I take his hand and simultaneously touch the body part that I am singing about. I do this so that one day without my direction he will remember and simultaneously touch the body part we are singing about.

God is the same way with us. When we are going through the storms of life he is singing, *Head . . . shoulders knees and toes.* He points to each part reminding us that we should know He is the *Head* of our lives. He won't make us *shoulder* more than we can bear. Stay on our *knees* and pray and He shall direct our path. As He points to our *eyes,* God wants us to remember to walk by faith and not by sight. God points to our *ears and mouth* reminding us not to listen to the report of the enemy, but to continue to speak life over ourselves and our situations because the power of life and death is in the tongue.

To our surprise God points to our hearts and says, **knows.** God explains that as His children we should **know** He is going to come through for us. Even when it looks and sounds like we have been beaten, our faith should remind us of all that He has already brought us through. We should **know** He is faithful and just to deliver us. He is the same God with the same delivering power today as He had in the bible days. God just wants us to get to the point where we can encourage ourselves and with expectancy smile in faith singing: eyes and ears mouth and **knows** head, shoulders **Knees** and toes....

Ayesha Z. Howard

He's An On-time God

Read Ecclesiastes 3:1 & Genesis 1: 6-15

To every thing there is a season, a time to every purpose under the heaven:

-Ecclesiastes 3:1

My wife and I recently took a mini vacation to the Poconos this past Memorial Day weekend. I tried to keep up with the same schedule as if I was at home. On Tuesday night we had Bible study just as I would at home; and in the morning I have my personal time with God.

For this I automatically wake up at 3:15 a.m. This is the time I meditate and talk with God. From time to time the hour may vary. If it's not 3:15 a.m., it's 3:30 a.m. Very rarely it goes to 4 a.m., and when I meditate I lose track of time. While I was on vacation I thought I might oversleep and miss my time with God because I'm away, relaxed and out of my normal surroundings. I was, therefore, amazed that at exactly 3:15 a.m. I awoke to meditate.

When I am deep into meditation at home I'm alerted to the sound of the birds chirping and breaking out into a song with several other birds joining in. By that sound I'm aware that it's between the hours of 4:00 a.m. and 5:00 a.m. When I meditated in the Poconos the sound of the birds alerted me again, and as I slowly opened my eyes I noticed that it was 4:40 a.m.

Not only did I come out of my meditation the same time I usually do, I noticed that all birds must be on the same time table, chirping at the same time no matter where you are. Only God could set this time table into motion. With my eyes fully opened I saw a mist or clouds hovering around the mountains as if it were a scene from Genesis 1: 6-15. This is a testimony that God is an on-time God.

No matter what you ask God for, He will work it out in His own time. Our time is not God's time; you may not get it when you want it, but He'll give it to you when you need it because He's an on-time God.

Father God, my times are in your hands. Keep me in tune with your will and teach me to wait on you.

- Edward Mack

Praying Is Still In Style

Read Matthew 6:9-13

Then you will call upon me and come and pray to me, and I will listen to you.

Jeremiah 29:12 NKJV

Growing up in Jamaica in my preteen was a wonderful experience, except for the daily routine of praying and reading the Bible after school—so I thought. It took me well into my late twenties to realize the only way to talk to God is by praying.

Praying has been taken out of American Public Schools. And almost out of the workplace where workers fear losing their job if they do. I've made it known on my job that I'm a Christian and the only man that I fear is God. Don't fear what man does to the earthly body but what God can do to the soul. So pray continually. (1 Thessalonians 5:17)

I find that praying is the best stress reliever, especially when praying as a family—even if there is only time for "Our Father." Because the temptation is so great with the Internet and television basically just waking each morning can lead to temptation. Matthew 26:41 says, "Watch and pray lest you enter into temptation. The spirit indeed is willing, but the flesh is weak."

If it were not for praying family and friends, I can honestly say I don't think Shauna and I would be where we are today: back together with four wonderful kids lifting up the name of Jesus, and celebrating our fifteenth wedding anniversary.

There is no long distance or roaming charge for praying. It's toll free 24/7. In the words of gospel singer, J. Moss: "Operator, get heaven on the line. Can you make a connection? I've got to call Him. There's something on my mind."

Praying will always be in style. Father, please help us to pray without ceasing.

- Ricardo Carty

Alone with God

Genesis 34: 24-28

So Jacob was left alone, and a man wrestled with him till daybreak . . . . But Jacob replied, "I will not let you go unless you bless me."

"Jacob was left alone." Can you recognize times in your life when you have been separated from family and friends in order to come face to face with God? Being alone can sometimes seem scary, but I pray that you can recognize that there are times when God needs time with just you to help you draw closer to Him.

"A man (God) wrestled with him till daybreak" Jacob wrestled with God all night long. Jacob may have been tired but he never stopped and he never gave up. There are times when you have to be like Jacob and never stop and never give up because your struggles and trials are what make you strong.

"He (God) touched the socket of Jacob's hip." In this verse God is showing you that He is all powerful. But even after his hip was wrenched, Jacob did not stop wrestling with God. Jacob said to God "I will not let go until you bless me." Jacob struggled all of his life. Yet, at that moment, Jacob had to realize what was worth holding on to... his struggles with his brother Esau, reentering Canaan, family issues or hold on to the one who holds his future.

You have to learn to let go of the right things. When the struggles in your life get hard you can't hold on to the same old stuff you always do because it's comfortable. You have to hold on to that which will make you stronger not weaker. At the end of Jacob's struggle, God changed his name. God has the power to change your name. What that means is that when you over come your struggles, you will no longer be the same!

Lord, please teach me how to let go of things in my life so that I may fully hold on to you. Lord, give me the strength to not let go until you bless me.

-Jennifer R. Jones

The Perfect Hook-up

Read Deuteronomy 28: 1-8

The LORD will command the blessings on you in your storehouses and in all to which you set your hand.

- Deuteronomy 28:8a

"It's not what you know but who you know" is an expression frequently used to sum up the criteria for finding success as defined by the world. Hence we find that the world puts a lot of emphasis on networking: making the right and most advantageous connections for the advancement of personal agendas.

As Christians **who** we know and **what** we know are both important. We know *Jesus Christ as Lord and Savior,* and we know that *"the gospel of Christ is the power of God unto salvation to everyone who believeth."* (Romans 1:16); and we know that Jesus wants to give us "a rich and satisfying life." (John 10:10, NLT). Our most advantageous connection—the perfect hook-up—is our relationship with Jesus Christ, and our fellowship with other believers. Our most effective net-working tools are fervent prayers, the Word of God, and the guidance of the Holy Spirit. Only God knows what our true potentials are and He is the only one who can arrange to have these potentials realized. "I know the plans I have for you," says the Lord. "They are plans for your good and not for disaster, to give you a future and a hope." (Jeremiah 29:11 NLT)

Whatever it is that you are pursuing: whether it is career goals, higher education, financial success, or general prosperity, you can rest assured that Jesus has you covered.

Stay in the Word and pray for courageous and consistent faith to continue living according to His will and purpose.

-Rosetta Jamieson-Thomas

Lord, I Come

I come…
With hardly a word to say
Just expecting a heart to heart
From my heart to yours
Your heart back to mine
I come, Lord

To feel your presence
To be comforted and reassured
Because I have a longing
A thirst to be satisfied
I come

As a young child
Seeking the warm embrace in her father's bosom
Wanting nothing
But needing everything
I come

Because I have been stretched beyond my physical limits feeling like
there is no elasticity left
Just about to burst
I come

Because although the sun goes down
And the sky darkens
The days never seem to end
They just roll along
So I come

In the mid night hour of one day
But also the break of another day
You encourage me to cast my cares upon you
Because you care for me
That's why I come

So here I am Lord
Yes, here I am
Welcome me, comfort me, embrace me, renew me, strengthen me,
Encourage me
Give me all that I need
Because you alone are God

- Ruth Skerritt-Abraham

Blessings of a Prayer Walk

Read Matthew 18: 18-20

He shall call upon me, and I will answer him: I will be with him in trouble: I will deliver him, and honor him. With long life will I satisfy him, and show him my salvation.

-Psalm 91:15-16

Reflect, for a moment, on the blessed privilege and power of prayer which God made available to us, through Jesus Christ, so that we may come boldly into His presence, and experience His grace and mercy. Isn't it awesome that God blesses us with His attention? His focus is on us. He listens and He hears us, and gives us the assurance of His answer.

On a beautiful Saturday morning in the summer a small group of us—women of God — met in our community park for prayer. The Prayer Walk was initiated by Carol Carter, President of the Women's Guild, and what a blessing it was! As we prayed and shared our thoughts and stories of faith we received the blessing of God's presence in a mighty way. *"For where two or three are gathered together in my name, I am there in the midst of them." Matthew 18:20*

We recognized the manifestation of His awesome power, His majesty, and His omnipotence in the beauty of His creation: the vast canopy of blue skies, drifting clouds, golden sunshine, wide open spaces, majestic hills, valleys, trees, — all things great and small — And man! That is, He created you and He created me. *"He has made the earth by His power. He has established the world by His wisdom, and has stretched out the heavens by His discretion."(Jeremiah 10:12).* There is nothing that our God cannot do.

As we continued our leisurely and meditative stroll through the park, we received the blessing of His peace in our hearts, and felt its manifestation in the cool, gentle breeze, in the tranquility of the lake, and in the serenity of the tree-lined trails we followed through the park. *"The Lord gives His people strength. The Lord blesses them with peace." (Psalm 29:11)*

As we ended our prayer walk and prepared to go home, we knew in our hearts, that God had touched each of us in a special way. We left the park with a song in our hearts, an acute awareness of His presence in our lives, and that deep feeling of peace and inner joy that only He can give.

Oh come let us sing unto the Lord; let us make a joyful noise to the rock of our salvation. (Psalm 95:1)

Jesus knew He would not always be physically present with His followers but His Spirit would abide with us. His presence is manifested through the presence of the Holy Ghost in our lives, but to grow in grace requires some initiative on our part. To experience His peace we must actively seek His presence, individually as well as in the fellowship of other believers. Like Mary, we must abide in His presence (Luke 10:27-43) and listen to His words.

These words from a well-known gospel song succinctly express the desire of our hearts: "Just a closer walk with Thee. Grant it, Jesus, is my plea. Daily walking close to Thee; Let it be, dear Lord, let it be".

-Rosetta Jamieson-Thomas

Testimonies

Read Luke 8: 26 -39

But Jesus sent him away saying, "Return to your own house, and tell what great things God has done for you."
And he went his way and proclaimed throughout the whole city what great things Jesus has done for him.

Luke 8: 38-39 (NKJV)

All Your work shall praise You, O Lord,
And Your saints shall bless you
They shall speak of the glory of Your kingdom,
And talk of your power.
To make known to the sons of men His mighty acts,
And the glorious majesty of His kingdom

Psalm 145: 10-12(NKJV)

Prayer Focus

Come and let us declare in Zion the work of the Lord our God.

Jeremiah 51:10b (NKJV).

Nothing Is Impossible With God

Read Proverbs 3:5-6

Now Faith is the substance of things hope for, the evidence of things not seen.-

-Hebrews 11:1

Recently I had a conversation with a young man who was depressed because of his financial difficulties. He was in the process of getting evicted from his apartment after being in arrears for paying rent. He had limited time to produce a down payment before the court could make any payment arrangements on his behalf. This young man became so distraught that he was considering talking to a loan-shark.

After we prayed for guidance and for faith in God I counseled him against dealing with a loan shark. Not only would he be getting deeper in debt, he would be putting his life in danger as well as bondage. Then I prayed that God would deliver him from the consequences of dealing with corrupt and depraved people with contaminating influences. After we prayed I asked him if he consulted with an attorney.

The man said that he called Legal Aid but they were booked until January of 2009. I guided him to call pre-paid legal service. Since he was in another state, most likely he would have to join over the phone (it takes about 10 min.) but at least he can get an immediate courtesy consultation. The young man took my advice and I learned that the attorney will handle the case. I thanked God that I was able to talk and pray with him so that his life would not be in jeopardy dealing with loan sharks.

Heavenly Father, I thank you for your guidance in all matters and again demonstrating that there is no problem, circumstance or situation greater than you.

Be careful for nothing; but in everything by prayer and supplication with thanksgiving let your requests be made known unto God.

- Ed. Mack

Through A Father's Eyes

A Prayer for Family Healing

Read James 5:13-20

The prayer of faith shall save the sick, and the Lord shall raise him up; and if he has committed sins, they shall be forgiven him.

–James 5:16

O Lord, you said our bodies are the Temple of your Holy Spirit. Lord, we desire to be in good health. We seek the truth that will make us free from stumbling and instill in us natural good habits. Father, you bought us at a very high price that you may be glorified. O God, we need healing. Father, we come before you asking for your healing power. Lord, we pray you raise us up and if we have committed any sins please forgive us and help us to let go of all unforgiving resentment, and anger, and bad feeling towards anyone. In the name of Jesus, Amen

Years ago when my daughter was infected with H.I.V. from her husband I was so angry I almost lost my soul forever. I bought a gun and left for the state in which they live, for the sole purpose of killing my son-in-law. But, Jesus intervened, and by His grace I found my God who gave me the power to forgive my son-in-law.

However, forgiveness was not an easy thing to do for she is my baby girl. I watched her suffer. I saw the light fade from her eyes as her body diminished. I suffered with her, and I prayed through our pain. I prayed day and night, for three to four months, and I know it was through the application of prayer that God put the light back in her eyes. When I saw it I fell on my face and gave God many praises, for I know it was God who gave her that victory look that was in her eyes.

My daughter has suffered much in her life, but in the midst of her suffering she has found a new joy, and her life is a blessing to me. I praise God for showering his blessings upon my daughter who I love so much. I praise God for using her life, and her suffering, to set me on the path to Jesus Christ who saved me and turned me away from my worldly life of sin.

The effectual fervent prayer of a righteous man availeth much.

– **Joseph Thompson**

God Fixes Broken Marriages

Read Psalm 127

"Unless the Lord builds the house, they labor in vain who build it... Behold, children are a heritage from the Lord, the fruit of the womb is a reward."

-Psalm 127:1, 3

God is able to sustain strong marriages and to repair broken marriages. He is also able to bless the childless with children.

My life was at a turning point in March 2000. I could have chosen job security and invested in my career. I had a Master's degree, no children, and a job that paid more than I needed to support myself. However, a single day of getting alone to read God's word and praying to Him for direction—praying and fasting—convicted me that I was to give up that job to reunite with my husband from whom I'd been separated for two years.

We tell this story again and again because again and again, we watch marriages around us fall apart. I didn't know where I was going to live, or where I was going to work, and Ricky had no concrete plans laid out for us. Yet, I felt unflinching conviction that God was telling me to trust Him and He would take care of me, and He has—exceedingly, abundantly above all that I would ever ask or think. Praise God in Jesus' name! Hallelujah! Thank you, Jesus!

I could not have foreseen life with our beautiful children, or watching my stepson graduate from high school and starting college. We're glad we trusted in the Lord!

God means what He says. He mends broken hearts and repairs broken marriages.

- **Shauna Carty**

The Light

Read Psalm 27

The LORD is my light and my salvation;
Whom shall I fear?
The LORD is the strength of my life;
Of whom shall I be afraid?

Many years ago
When I was going through difficult times
The LORD led me to Psalm Twenty-seven.

When I was in distress
And could not find my way
I heard, ***"Follow the Light."***

When I was overwhelmed
By everyday burdens
I heard, ***"Come to the Light."***

When I called on Jesus
And prayed
And asked for help
I heard, ***"I Am the LIGHT"***

Therefore I will offer sacrifices of joy in His tabernacle
I will sing, yes, I will sing praises to the LORD.

                                    - Catherine Williams

This devotional is dedicated to my precious sister, Myra Carolyn Nelson, who saw that magnificent sunset with me in New Mexico. Myra suddenly passed on April 28, 2009. I will forever carry her memory in my heart.

It's Later Than You Think!

A Personal Testimony

"To every thing there is a Season, a time to every purpose under the Heaven."

Ecclesiastes 3:1

As I focus on telling my personal truth for the Thanksgiving Season, I am very grateful for so many things in my life. Even when difficulties and trials arise, I am convinced that it's only for a season — for I know that the best day of my life is today; and when I quietly fall asleep tonight, I relish in the excitement knowing that tomorrow will be my best day. When I reflect upon, "For this is the day that the Lord has made…," my hope is transcended into an optimism that I sometimes find difficult to verbalize.

My cancer diagnosis in 2006, and a frightening repeat threat of its return revealed by a MRI and CT Scan a year later, strongly compelled me to get my house in order, so to say. Thanks to God, the abnormalities found in my body were just a false scare. Although I was told by my oncologist that the daily drug I take is still working, but in my heart of hearts, I knew that it was the Divine Interventionist giving me a second chance.

As I reflect upon the devastation that is taking place all around us — that is —millions of people in this country who have been tremendously impacted by our economy's all time low (myself included in this growing number. After 35 years of working in the corporate world, I was downsized by a massive layoff.) We have people who do not know where their next meal is coming from; a homeless population that is enormously growing by the tens of thousands with the mortgage foreclosure crisis. We have a nation at war with soldiers not returning home, and those who are returning are coming home to a system that has economically failed them and their families. We have millions who are without healthcare; and through these tragic crises, we have many of our senior population who are isolated and lonely, subsequently, leaving too many suffering with debilitating bouts of depression.

It's difficult for me not to feel sadness; but I try my best to redirect my energies from fear and sadness to those areas where I am capable in making a positive difference. As a cancer survivor and a professional human relations specialist, I have come to understand human hurt and what pure rage feels like. Although I am a firm believer that "purpose" finds you, and not the other way around, I believe that the Divine Plan is continuously unfolding as the many turns of events in my life put me in touch with that divine idea and "purpose."

One of those times came a year after my diagnosis as I watched the most magnificent sunset over the majestic mountains in one of America's beautiful southwestern cities. It was late evening as my husband and I (along with my two sisters and their husbands) silently drove through the dessert of the Old Route 66 Highway after a long day of immersing ourselves in the rich culture and exploring Albuquerque, New Mexico. It was then I begin to realize that God's plan is simple; not complicated in any way; and this unhurried precious time somehow made me feel nurtured, validated, and better about myself. I felt God just wanted me to get in touch with that higher intelligence within and listen—just quietly listen for His wisdom.

So each Thanksgiving Season, I am grateful for the turning points and many lessons God has unfolded. Would I have learned these lessons without cancer? That answer remains unknown, although it certainly was a re-defining moment in my life. Consequently, after the confrontation with my mortality, I finally have learned to accept death as a part of life, to celebrate each new Season, and to blaze my own path. I strongly encourage you to do the same because it's much later than you think!

> *"The tragedy of life is not that it ends so soon,*
> *But we wait so long to begin it!"*
> -Unknown

- **Linda McQuilla-Jones**

The Power of Prayer

And all things, whatsoever ye shall ask in prayer, believing, ye shall receive".

Matthew 21:22

The year was 1997, and as I was jogging around the track my chest felt tight. I noticed that I was breathing heavier than usual. Suddenly I fell to my knees gasping for air. As I walked ever so slowly home, I decided to call my doctor and he advised me to come into his office. When I arrived, his nurse asked me to come into the examination room. I was already nervous because this was an experience I never encountered.

As my doctor listened to my chest he stopped asked me to cough and continued to listen. He decided to send me to get an x-ray of my chest. After the lab technician reviewed the x-ray he said, "You better go back to your doctor's office your left lung looks like a deflated balloon." As I returned to my doctor's office he was waiting patiently. The lab technician must have already called him and told him that I was on my way.

My doctor told me that I had a collapsed lung and he needed to admit me into the hospital immediately. Well, this really blew my mind because as I explained to my doctor, I had driven to the hospital and my car was parked in the lot across the street; the bill would be enormous. My doctor stated that if I thought I could make it home that would be fine. It would take time to get me a room in the hospital and I would be called when a room was ready.

Upon arriving at the hospital and checking in (call it fear of being in the hospital because I never was) I noticed that my symptoms worsened and I required oxygen. Then the turn for the worse came. The staff began to prep me for tubes to inflate my lungs. What happed after that was like a nightmare. The tubes that were inserted into my lungs caused an infection, and I went from bad to worse.

After days had gone by and I was not improving, I had several prayer vigils at my bedside from members of my church, at that time. My pastor was there everyday. The doctors told my family that it

99

didn't look good for me and they felt I was giving up. As a matter of fact, I wasn't giving up; I was just tired of being probed. Throughout this six-week ordeal, I was sedated for most of the time. One day, my Pastor was in my room and I was told while I was sedated I started to recite the names of God in Hebrew. My Pastor, who was also my teacher and mentor, stated that I said the names of God better than I did in class.

I was told that the doctor just sat back in the chair until I was finish calling out to God, hoping I was finished before the sedative wore off. Four days later and after so many prayers from the Saints of God I started to improve. My fever broke, the infection was eradicated, and my appetite returned. I made a major improvement. Prior to this I was on liquids only and went from 195 lbs to 145lbs. The doctors were amazed at my 360 degree turn around. My personal physician told me that I must have had Jesus on my side because at one point he thought he was going to lose me. He then said that he believed all those prayers worked and I had a better physician then him, named Jesus.

Father God in the name of Jesus, I believed that I am healed, according to 1 Peter 2:24. "Who his own self bare our sins in his own body on the tree that we, being dead to sins, should live unto righteousness: by whose stripes we were healed".

- Edward Mack

Reflections

Read Philippians 4:1-8

Finally, brethren, what ever things are true, whatever things are noble, whatever things are just, whatever things are pure, whatever things are lovely, whatever things are of good report, if there is any virtue and if there is anything praiseworthy — meditate on these things

Philippians 4:8

Do not be conformed to this world, but be transformed by the renewing of your mind, that you may prove what is the good, and acceptable, and perfect will of God.

Romans 12:2

Prayer Focus

You will keep him in perfect peace, whose mind is stayed on you, because he trusts in you

Isaiah 26: 3

Light of the World
-Christmas Reflections

Read Matthew 1: 18-25

Then Jesus spoke to them again saying, "I am the light of the world. He who follows me shall not walk in darkness, but have the light of life."

-John 8:12 NKJV

Christmas has become so commercialized that it becomes difficult, especially when you have children, to avoid being caught up in the commercial mayhem . . . .

"Grandma, we put up our Christmas tree today."

"Did you get a gift for so and so . . .?"

"Finish shopping yet?"

"Are you going to the tree-lighting ceremony?"

I drive through my neighborhood. Houses are aglow with festive Christmas lights – from the rooftops to the lawns below. As I pull into my driveway, my husband is busily stringing red and green lights from our front door to the shrubs growing along the side of our house.

"Honey, we need to buy some more lights. Many of these don't work anymore."

Festive holiday lights are among the best selling and most sought after commodity at Christmas time, and the Christmas tree has become one of the world's most significant symbols of Christmas.

As Christians, we can enjoy the festive atmosphere created by Christmas decorations. However, we do not need a festive Christmas tree and myriads of lights glowing and twinkling on our lawns to experience the joy and peace of Christmas. Jesus is the light of the world. He is the reason we celebrate Christmas. Day by day our lives must "bear witness of that Light."

Let the love, peace and joy of knowing Jesus as Lord and Savior radiate from your hearts and homes to light the paths and warm the hearts and homes of others. Keep **Christ,** the Light of the World, in **Christ**mas.

Father God, help us to walk always as children of light to the honor and glory of your name. Amen.

- Rosetta Jamieson-Thomas

But Now I See

Read Psalm 27 & Mark 5:1-20

I had fainted, unless I had believed to see the goodness of the LORD in the land of the living.

-Psalm 27:13

When he saw Jesus from a distance, he ran and fell on his knees in front of him

- Mark 5:6

"I had fainted, unless..." Wow where would I be if it were not for that "Unless, I Had Believed." Thank you Jesus that I believed— no I mean Believe— that I would see the goodness of the Lord in the land of the living.

For years I thought I had to die or take my own life in order to feel the goodness of the Lord or to feel the true peace of His presence. But No! In Psalm 27:13 God has told me that I will see the goodness of the Lord in the land of the living. God's word did not say "know the goodness" because if you know something then where is the demonstration of your faith? God's word did not say "feel the goodness" because feelings change; feelings are never constant. God said "SEE". I once was blind but now I SEE... oh to behold the Lord through my own eyes right now, right now in the land of the living.

During Saul's conversion, in Acts 9:9, Saul was struck blind after speaking with the Lord, but three days later, "Thank you Jesus", he was made whole and he could SEE. Saul's whole outlook on life changed once God restored his sight. Another story can be found in Mark 5:1-20; specifically Mark 5:6 "But when he saw Jesus a far off, he ran and worshipped Him." Many preachers have said the demon possessed man ran to Jesus because the demons were afraid of Jesus. But here's what I take from it...

For me, for years and years such a big part of me wanted to die. I couldn't stand being in my own skin. The devil had me bamboozled thinking that I could only be free with the Lord if I take my own life. But yet there was a part of me that wanted to live. A part of me wanted to reach out and take hold of God. That demon possessed man spent years and years being bamboozled by the devil. We were both going through life BLIND.

But then one day... I'm going to write that again... There came a day when JESUS was a far off but the man SAW Jesus. He fell to his knees and worshipped him. Oh to SEE Jesus, to SEE Jesus, to SEE Jesus a far off and recognize that there is still goodness here in the land of the living. To SEE Jesus and run to Him, fall at his feet, and worship Him.

Even though the man had been possessed for years and years, and saw nothing but dark caves and the wounds on his body that he inflicted on himself, there was still a part of him that had hope because he SAW Jesus. The demon possessed man did not run back into the caves. He didn't try to take his life... no he ran towards Jesus. From there the demons were cast out by Jesus and the man sat there clothed and in his right mind.

Where did the change happen? It was the instant he SAW Jesus and he decided to run toward Him and not away from Him. "I would have fainted" Fainted = Given Up = Gave in = Cared less = Turned Away = Died... "unless, I had believed to SEE the goodness of the Lord in the land of the living." We serve a Living God. Now its time to let him live in us. Let Him live in you.

Lord, live in us. Let us See You. Open our eyes as only you can so that we might gaze upon your goodness and run to you.

"Was blind but NOW I SEE" It is time for you to go from the "Caves" of your life that represent Darkness to "SEEING" all that Jesus has for you. It is never too late to SEE Jesus and make the decision to run to Him.

-Jennifer R. Jones

Parenting 101

Read James 1:2-4

Train up a child in the way he should go, and when he is old he will not depart from it.

–Proverbs 22:6

We always say that children do not come with a parenting handbook. But I beg to differ; we have the BIBLE – **B**asic **I**nstruction **B**efore **L**eaving **E**arth. The Bible instructs us to "train up a child in the way he should go, and when he is old he will not depart from it."

We are given many examples of good and bad parenting: Job and his children, Joshua and his household, Aaron and his sons, Samuel and his sons, Jacob and his sons, Eli and his sons and many more. Ultimately, we can instruct our children regarding the things of the Lord but must understand that the choice is theirs. My oldest son said to me the other day that it was too difficult trying to decide whether to do the right thing, and truly I understand the dilemma. Whether you are a child or an adult "choice" always presents itself.

As much as we would like to walk our children through the maze of life and physically steer them through the turns, that's not realistic. But I encourage you today in that the scripture says, "…, but we glory in tribulations also: knowing that tribulation worketh patience; and patience, experience; and experience, hope" (Romans 5:3-4) They must go through something. How do you know what you are able to endure if you were never faced with hardship? Then you will only be able to give an account about what someone else's experience. "Blessed is the man that endureth temptation: for when he is tried, he shall receive the crown of life, which the Lord hath promised to them that love him." (James 1:12)

Therefore, Parenting 101 – train the children in the ways of the Lord; teach them to endure for the sake of our Heavenly Father because that builds character and shows integrity. Our perfect example is Jesus and His Father. Jesus was tempted in every aspect but did not sin. When Jesus went through that humiliating experience on the cross, He felt for a moment that His Heavenly Father had deserted him, but His father knew that He had taught him well. It was the will of God that He endures the cross for the redemption of your sins and mine.

So let's teach our children to pray: "Our Father which art in Heaven ... Thy Kingdom come, thy will be done on earth as it is in Heaven".

– Ruth Skerritt-Abraham

Role Models

Read 2 Samuels 6: 13-15

And David danced before the LORD with all his might.

2 Samuels 6:14a

When you think of the word *model* do you think about the runway, or do you think about your life style? Are you modeling your ways after the Lord or the world?

So many times we follow after those who we think are so hot, but in actuality they are not. God does not want us to be clones. He has created us to be unique individuals in Him. He has formed us in His likeness so, we should start modeling righteousness. Do you know that no two persons on this earth have the same exact finger print! Who could orchestrate that but the Lord!

Are we going to be the ones that become those **Holy** role models in someone else's life, or will we continue to sit back and allow the world to temporarily steal the spotlight? Brothers and sisters you'd better model!

God has done so much for me, so "when the Spirit of the Lord comes upon my heart, I will dance like David danced".

-Marissa Moore

The Vision

Give her of the fruit of her hands . . .
Proverbs 31:31a

Many years ago, as I lay praying unto The Lord, He took me into a deep sleep and began to show me a vision. I could see a field; it appeared to be a playground. The playground was endless. As The Lord showed me more, children filled the field—from diaper-clad infants on up. They begin to cry out all at once. "A cry in the wilderness" . . . if you will. I stretched forth my hand to comfort them, and their voices would not be stilled. The cries grew louder. My spirit began to cry out in response to their cries, and then, I was awakened by the Lord. God interpreted that vision a few days hence. Not long after, God spoke to my heart during Bible study and said to return to Second Baptist Church.

The fruit—spiritual sons and daughters called to prophesy, proclaim and publish. Nieces, nephews, God-children.... bounty! There is also fruit that satan tries to pluck from The Vine—Part of "the first-fruit", in fact. Some blooming, budding, producing. Others prodigal, lost, or "in labor and delivery", and The Great Physician must be called on, Stat! Fruit. Yet, the Lord has been our dwelling place from generation unto generation.

The Lord has called us into the harvest, as laborers. Multitudes upon multitudes still stand in the valley of indecision, while others are ripe and ready to drawn unto salvation. Continue to plant, continue to water. The increase of God is nigh.

All of you make a difference in my life, and an impact upon my eternity. Love You.

–Barbara D. Turner

Mother/Father Tribute

A tribute to Gwen LeGrand from her son on Father's Day

I can do all things through Christ who strengthens me.

- Philippians 4:13)

strong single mother
provides three kids a home
bypassing all the day's struggles
raising three small kids
in a fatherless home
silently crying alone

day in, day out
she cooks, she cleans
all the while supporting their dreams

then cancer strikes thrice
and each time hits harder
now who will provide for the kids?

extremely weak from the chemo
feeling battered and bruised
she hides the pain from her young

Mother/father fights harder
and teaches them all
to do what she can do no longer
now (they) kids cook and clean
wash their own cloths
and do the same for mother/father

three youth imposters
act as adults
as they learned from mother/father

playing both roles
in a single parent home
mother/father never complained

never missing a father
never going without
kids were loved without a doubt

I will raise my girls
as I learned from my mother
and try to explain it to them

how though it was hard
how you still pushed on
and how you never thought to give in

I will teach them to cook
teach them to clean
and share all I've learned from you

they will know right from wrong
and will always press on
just as you showed us to
women can't raise men
people yell all the time
I will debate that to the end
I am now a man
from a fatherless home
for that I give thanks to my mom

- Jubair LeGrand

Poor But Blessed

Read Luke 6:20-25

"For it is easier for a camel to go through the eye of a needle than for a rich man to enter the kingdom of God."

-Luke 18:25 NKJV

"God desires us to be rich," a religious leader told the audience of the radio program on which he was being interviewed recently. He went on to say that people often ask him why is it that they are spiritually saved, but they are not prospering financially. He then summarized a popular message that is being preached from many pulpits today. That message is that salvation through Jesus Christ leads to prosperity.

Not necessarily. Jesus tells us to "...seek first the kingdom of God and His righteousness and all these things shall be added to you." (Matthew 6:33) Apostle Paul writes, "And my God shall supply all your need according to His riches in glory by Christ Jesus." (Philippians 4:19) Those two verses from the Bible, among others, can be interpreted to mean that God will bless us financially. Yet, when I consider them in the context of Jesus' love for the poor, I conclude that salvation can go hand in hand with poverty, but the poor will be blessed.

Jesus' love for the poor is shown repeatedly in the Bible. He told a rich ruler who practiced keeping all the commandments that he lacked one thing for him to inherit eternal life. "Sell all that you have and distribute to the poor, and you will have treasure in heaven; and come, follow Me." (Luke 18:22)

Jesus likens himself to the poor. He talks about separating people into two groups when He returns. One group will inherit the kingdom of God and the other will be cast into the everlasting fire prepared for the devil and his angels (Matthew 25:34 and 41). Why? The first will be rewarded for taking care of the poor, and the second will be punished for neglecting the poor. Jesus refers to poor people in the first person. He says, "for I was hungry and you gave

111

me food…" (Matthew 25:35). He adds, "…inasmuch as you did it to one of the least of these My brethren, you did it to Me." (Matthew 25:40).

Father, please help us to seek you for our spiritual health instead of financial wealth, and to serve the poorest and weakest brethren.

– Ricardo and Shauna Carty

Disappointed or Expected?
Parable of the Talents

Read Matthew 25:14-30

His Lord said to him, ". . . . you have been faithful over a few things, I will make you ruler over many things . . . ."

Matthew 25:23

What do you do when you are disappointed? Should your expectations be lowered all around? Should you even have expectations?

When a person disappoints you or lets you down, that should be a reminder that **no** human being is 100% dependable. All of your trust should not be placed in humanity anyway. I have heard the following phrase come across a number of pulpits in the church: "You can never fully trust man because man will fail you."

The aforementioned quote says a lot to the capabilities of humanity. For the most part, people want to be considered trustworthy and dependable, and when they fail to be so at one time or another, others tend to lose faith in them. Does that take something away from a person's credibility? In the world and according to its standards, the answer is "yes". On the other hand, from the onset, God's standards and methodologies are different.

As the Creator of all living beings, God knows what we are capable of and what we are not. The Book of Job records the following concerning God and humanity, "Shall mortal man be more just than God? Shall a man be more pure than his maker? Behold, He put no trust in His servants; and His angels He charged with folly:" (Job 4:17-18) If we were made "a little lower than the angels," (Hebrews 2:7) how much of our wisdom and actions are considered more than folly?

Now, consider the example of the talents, in the Gospel of Matthew 25:14-30. Here, the servant who had little entrusted to him got that taken away. What does this say about the master's expectations? He must not have expected too much of the worker since he was entrusted with so little. In the same token, he who was given much, invested in what he had, and *then* was given *more!*

God starts off trusting us with little, then once we prove to be "faithful over the few things, He makes us ruler over many." (Matthew 25:23) In these cases, the world operates from a backwards standpoint, as compared to the way God operates.

In taking on the characteristics of Christ, our attitudes and actions should be the same. This might be taking a chance, but if we *expect* people to fail, when they succeed in faithfulness and dependability, we can raise our expectations of them. Why not give it a shot?

-Marette A. Moore

Little Time, Little Peace, Little Joy

Read Ecclesiastes 3:1-8; John 14:27

To everything there is a season, A time for every purpose under the sun.

Ecclesiastes 3:1

Our lives consist of little time as found in Ecclesiastes 3:1 which God showers down upon us. Time never stands still; it continues to move constantly around us. We must never stop trying to make the best of the time God gives us by serving Him. Not just serving, but giving the very best of our service to the one and only God of our salvation. Then and only then will we find a little peace, as found in John 14:27.

When peace is in our lives, it makes life worth living and keeps us headed in the right direction. God said, "My peace I give unto you." Where God's peace is, there is happiness that causes us to want to run on and see what the end will be. That peace of God that makes us want to praise and serve God with all our hearts, mind and soul.

With the peace of God in our hearts, we can have joy. Joy in knowing that God is all that one needs to live with peace of mind and the mind to serve God. For the life of Christian joy to do any real good, it must be shared with others. We must sing his praises; we must exalt his name, we must share his story, and we must spread His joy. For the life of Christian joy to do any real good in a world full of people who wonder if Christ really makes a difference, our lives full of Christian joy must convince them.

To God be the glory for the time, peace and joy that can fill each heart and mind.

-Mollie Davis

Seeking the Center of Gravity

But they that wait upon the LORD shall renew their strength;
they shall mount up with wings as eagles; they shall run, and not be
weary; and they shall walk, and not faint.

ISAIAH **40:31**

As I reflect, I find that so many life-changing and challenging situations have occurred over the past ten years over my life's journey. These challenges have taken both sets of parents (mine and my husband's) to eternal life, along with most of all our first generation Mainliners; and sadly, far too many of our younger generation family members. My husband and I, through many years of burning the mid-night oil, finally completed our higher educational degrees that we sought to earn most of our lives, while working long hours to support ourselves and our children. And through many prayers, sweat and tears, although we were blessed with two good, God-fearing daughters, yes, there were tears at times because the parenting journey can get difficult with parental admonition about things as you try to teach the many life lessons. In the long run, through God's patience and help, we finally launched two beautiful daughters who have successfully established their own personal and professional lives.

Consequently, as I continue to keep God at the center of my life, I realize that seeking the center of my gravity has taken time — through both spiritual and personal reflection, and, at times, even painful reflection as I continue to assess and reassess my life. As I learn to renew myself after encountering the empty nest syndrome, suddenly being impacted by a corporate forced retirement, dealing with unanticipated health challenges, and suddenly losing my beloved sister of fifty-seven years, I desperately asked God to help me face this total life reorientation; and to find the emotional nourishment needed to face this uncomfortable middle year stage of my life.

Through many months of solitude and contemplation, and learning to live a life of enriching simplicity, my Heavenly Father, the source of my strength and salvation, has given me the foundation to retain my center. He has renewed my mind by giving me enriching ways in thinking, planning, and re-creating this very special time in these middle years. Once again, I am finding the serenity as I seek the center of gravity in my new life's evolution. What an exciting and productive time!

"Looking unto Jesus the author and finisher of our faith...."

-Linda McQuilla-Jones

I Will Fly Away
-Remembering Mama

Read Psalm 55: 1-6; John 14:1-4

And I said, "Oh that I had wings like a dove! For then would I fly away, and be at rest."

Psalm 55:6

One Sunday as the congregation sang the hymn, "Some bright morning when this life is over/ I'll fly away/ To a home on God's celestial shore / I'll fly away" I had a vivid flashback to my childhood and the woman who raised me as her own daughter when my natural mother walked away: my stepmother (Mama); "Miss Annie" to the neighbors; "Sister James" to the brethren of her congregation; "Grandma", to my children; the woman for whom my grand-daughter is named.

She was a direct descendant of the Maroons, a band of ex-slaves who escaped from the sugar plantations to the hills of Jamaica and courageously resisted the British colonial masters who settled on the island. She did not know her own parents; had no formal education; at an early age she became a seasoned "house maid" who took on the surname of the family for whom she worked. Hers was not an easy life. Yet, despite the hardship that fostered her early life, and the struggles that characterized her later life, her heart was full of love, joy, and kindness to others. No matter what challenges life threw her way, she would say, "The Lord will make a way." She never ceased to give thanks to God. She thanked Him for what she had; for what she didn't have; and for what she expected to have.

She was a strong woman – a woman of mountain-moving faith – who truly believed that one day she would fly away to Jesus. It was her life-long belief. She lived and breathed this belief, and as she aged and her physical strength declined she clung to that hope and longed for rest. I can still hear her voice in my head as she moved about singing, "If I had a wing like a dove, I'd fly, fly away and be at rest." Then one day, at age ninety-seven, that hope became her reality. She got her wings!

It took me years of spiritual growth to begin to understand her simple faith and trust in the Lord, and why and how she could've prayed those 'never-ending' payers. She had a relationship with Jesus!

Is life getting you down? Are you struggling to make ends meet? Is your mind filled with memories of loved ones who have passed on? Are you confronting the reality of your own mortality? "Let not your heart be troubled . . . ." Lean on Jesus and embrace the blessed hope that He has given us.

I thank you, Jesus, that you are taking care of our earthly needs; that you're gone to prepare a place for us, and that You will come back to receive us unto Yourself.

- Rosetta Jamieson-Thomas

Meet the Writers

1 Corinthians 2: 1-12

This publication, Green Pastures, is made possible through the power of the Holy Spirit, and is the combined efforts of the SBC Christian Writers Ministry members and other members of Second Baptist Church.

We write, "not with enticing words of man's wisdom, but in demonstration of the Spirit and of power: That your faith should not stand in the wisdom of men, but in the power of God. . . . Now we have received, not the spirit of the world, but the Spirit which is of God; that we might know the things that are freely given to us of God."

1 Corinthians 2: 4, 5, 12

Vicie Carter is a resident of Union, New Jersey. She is a widower, mother, grandmother, and cancer survivor who holds a Bachelors Degree in Theology. She has also served in various leadership capacities in her former church. Presently, she is the chaplain of the Prison Ministry, and a member of the Missionary Ministry of the Second Baptist Church in Roselle, New Jersey. Her favorite scripture is Matthew 6:33 (KJV): *But seek first the kingdom of God, and His righteousness; and all these things shall be added unto you.* Vicie Carter said, "To me this means that God wants to be first in every area of our life. He must come before our families, our jobs, and our possessions. When we obey God's commandments, everything that we do will fall in line with the plan that God has for our lives."

Annie Alexis Carty is the eight-year-old daughter of Ricardo and Shauna Carty, and grand-daughter of Rosetta Jamieson-Thomas. Annie loves the Lord and has given her life to Him. She is in the Fourth Grade. She loves to write, read, and play the piano. She attends Sunday School, sings with the Junior Choir, participates in the Liturgical Dance Ministry, and the Etiquette Ministry.

Ricardo & Shauna Carty penned their first "By Faith" in November 2001 to describe the miracle that God had worked in their lives. God reunited Ricky and Shauna after a two-year separation during which they moved as far apart as Florida is from New York, and each felt destined for divorce. "He removed the anger, resentment, and hurt from our hearts that had covered up the love that brought us together in the first place," they wrote in that first issue of "By Faith." This publication has since become a monthly reminder that we can do all things through Christ Jesus (Philippians 4:13). Prior to their separation, Ricky and Shauna had been married for four years, and had no children together. In June 2009, Ricky & Shauna celebrated their fifteenth wedding anniversary; praise God in Jesus' name! They live in Roselle, New Jersey with three of their children. Ricky's older son attends college. The family celebrates Jesus on Sunday mornings at Second Baptist Church.

Reverend Dr. Mollie Davis - wife, mother, grandmother – is a recipient of two Doctorate Degrees in Theology and Divinity from

Eastern Bible College. She is an Assistant Pastor at Second Baptist Church, Roselle; a Missionary, the Spiritual Advisor to several church auxiliaries, and an active member of the Interfaith Council. Lovingly called *The General*, she has a passion for service. In addition to preaching and teaching the Word of God, she cares for the homeless and senior citizens, administering to both their physical and spiritual needs.

Minister Alexis Hardy grew up in the Canarsie section of Brooklyn, New York. He gave his life to the Lord in 1997. Minister Hardy is married with two children and two grandchildren. He works with the youth, training boys to become godly men in the Boys to Men Ministry. He takes the Gospel of Christ to the streets through participation in the Mustard Seed Street Evangelism Ministry.

Evangelist Deborah Hardy loves the Lord Jesus Christ and has placed all of her trust in Him. She is a wife, mother, and grandmother, and resides in New Jersey with her family. She has been involved in the Prison Ministry for more than 10 years, and teaches Sunday School. She is co-leader of the Mustard Seed Street Evangelism Ministry. Evangelist Hardy works with the youth and sings in the choir. She has a tremendous love for God and a unique ministry — rightly dividing the Word of Truth as God allows her.

Ayesha Z. Howard, MSW, is a graduate of Columbia University School of Social Work. She loves the Lord Jesus Christ and is involved in the Young Adult Ministry. She writes poetry, and she enjoys dramatic reading, and liturgical dance. Ayesha has a way with words, and her poems are always a source of blessing and inspiration to others.

Rosetta Jamieson-Thomas is a Jamaican author and educator with degrees in Education and Creative Writing. She lives in Roselle, New Jersey. She is a member of Christian Writers Fellowship International, has published two novels: *Centre of the Labyrinth* and *A Margin of Hope*, and she is currently working on another. Rosetta loves the Lord Jesus Christ and has dedicated her teaching and writing to His glory. As the founder and facilitator of Second Baptist

Christian Writers Ministry, Roselle, New Jersey, she supports and encourages aspiring writers to develop and use their writing skills in the Ministry of the Gospel of Christ. Visit her at: http://www.rosettajthomas.com

Linda McQuilla-Jones, M.Ed., Ed.S., a Counselor Educator and a professional Mental Health Counselor, is known for her expertise in designing and facilitating seminars in Life-Style Management and Leadership. Linda is the wife of Barry Jones, and the proud mother of two professionally launched daughters, Jennifer and Vanessa Jones. Linda is a member of Second Baptist Church and serves as a Sunday School Teacher, a committee member in the Christian Writers Ministry and Assistant Editor of *Green Pastures*. Linda is on the Executive Board of the New Jersey Mental Health Counselors Association.

Linda's personal motto: Be the best at whatever you do.

Jennifer R. Jones, MA, NCC, is dedicated to using her testimony to reach and empower today's youth. Jennifer holds a Bachelor's Degree in Psychology and Studies of Women and Gender from The University of Virginia, and a Master's Degree in Community and School Counseling from Regent University. She is currently pursuing her Doctorate Degree in School Psychology at Rutgers University. Jennifer is choreographer for Anointed Spirits Praise Dancers at Second Baptist Church.

Jubair LeGrand is the 37 year-old son of Gwendolyn LeGrand. Jubair loves his mother and pays tribute to her for raising him to be the man he is today. He has a Bachelor of Science degree in Computer Engineering from New Jersey Institute of Technology (NJIT), and he works as a Test Lead for a multi-million dollar government contracting project. Jubair has two beautiful daughters who mean the world to him, and he is making every effort to raise them as he was raised. Daily he gives thanks to God for having a mother who loves the Lord and her children.

Deacon Edward Mack has been saved by Our Lord and Savior Jesus Christ for 23 years. Born in the Bronx, New York, married with four adult children, Deacon Ed and his wife Vernell reside in Roselle, New Jersey. He graduated from Huge Theological Institute in New York with a Masters Degree in Theology. Called to serve as a Deacon in 1994, he was re-ordained at Second Baptist Church in Roselle, New Jersey on November 25, 2007. Deacon Ed is a faithful servant of the Lord and a diligent student of His Word. He teaches Sunday School, is actively involved in the Christian Writers Ministry, and several other ministries at Second Baptist Church. He finds joy in serving and helping others through The Word.

Deacon Billy McDowell was born in Snow Hill, North Carolina. His love for singing praises unto God was nurtured at an early age when he sang in a choral ensemble with his siblings. Since joining Second Baptist in   1997, Deacon McDowell serves as Director of the Male Chorus, is a member of the Mass Choir, serves on the Diaconate Ministry, and is a Sunday School teacher. He loves serving the Lord alongside his lovely wife, Deaconess Starr McDowell.

Reverend James E. Moore, Sr., Pastor is a resident of Roselle, New Jersey for over 50 years, and Pastor of Second Baptist Church for ten years. Under Pastor Moore's leadership, the church family continues to grow spiritually and in numbers. He is truly an anointed man of God who loves the Lord and cares deeply for others. Not only does he minister to the needs of his congregation, he constantly reaches out to the wider community, and ministers to all as the Lord leads. A blessed family man, Pastor Moore is married to First Lady/Minister Margaret, and is the father of five children: Minister James, Jr., Marette, Marissa, Timothy and Tiffany.

First Lady, Minister Margaret Moore is the wife of Pastor James E. Moore, Sr., and a mother of five. She dedicated her life to the Lord in her early teens and has not looked back. She supports her pastor and husband in prayer and ministry. Minister Margaret was licensed as a Minister in 2003 and has been "provoking the people of God to good works" as the Word of God declares. She facilitates the Women's Breakfast Bible Study and is active in various ministries throughout the church body.

Minister James E. Moore, Jr. is a native of Roselle. Growing up as a preacher's child he gave his heart to God at an early age; and after a few of life's valuable lessons, he developed a closer relationship with the Lord in his adult years. After several years of avoiding the call to ministry, he submitted to God's voice and, in 2004, was licensed as a Minister. He continues to follow God's lead — preaching the Word as the opportunity presents. He is co-leader of the Young Adult Ministry and has served in this capacity for over five years.

Marissa Moore is the third child of Pastor James & Minister Margaret Moore. Marissa has four siblings and enjoys the fellowship that they have with one another. She also enjoys spending time with her church family. She has been involved in various ministries at the Second Baptist Church. This includes: singing in the choirs, singing on the Praise & Worship Team, dancing in the Liturgical Dance Ministry, assisting with the Drill Team and so much more. In May 2009 Marissa graduated from Union County College with an Associate of Arts Degree in Fine Arts (Drama). In September 2009, she ventured off to attend The Richard Stockton College, and is pursuing a Bachelor of Art degree in Theater Performance. Marissa enjoys participating in her college's Christian Fellowship groups, the Gospel Choir, and working on theater projects. She loves to bring joy to people's hearts through the gifts God has given her: acting, singing and dancing. Marissa hopes to be performing on Broadway someday and use her talents for the Lord's Glory. At twenty-four Marissa wants others to know that if they give God the best years of their lives, He will in turn do wonders through them. Marissa's favorite verse of scripture is, *Let no man despise thy youth; but be thou an example of the believers, in word, in conversation, in charity, in spirit, in faith, in purity. (1 Timothy 4:12)*

Marette A. Moore is the eldest daughter of the Moore family and is passionate about youth and music. She graduated from Rutgers University where she earned a Bachelor of Arts Degree in English, and a Master of Divinity Degree from New Brunswick Theological College, New Jersey. Marette has worked in public and private schools in the community, and is currently a Minister-in-Training and a worship leader at Abundant Life Family Worship Church in New Brunswick.

Yonette Morrison has Business Degrees from Rutgers University and a certificate from Cornell. She enjoys sightseeing, reading, and loves to spend time alone with God in meditation. She gave her life to the Lord at eleven years old and is very active in the children's ministry. In addition, she is responsible for the devotional ministry at her church. She is married and has one son. Above all, she wishes that this book of devotionals will be a tremendous blessing to our readers.

Evangelist Marilyn Poole is a mother of one son and grandmother of two, who loves the Lord with all that is within her. She is a health service provider specializing in senior care. Have a conversation with Evangelist Poole, and you'll see and hear the joy of the Lord coming from within her. Evangelist Poole became a licensed Minister of the Gospel in 2006. She has a distinct ministry style as she delivers the unadulterated Word of God in a most powerful way, as the Spirit leads.

Ruth Skerritt-Abraham is a devoted wife, aunt, and mother of five who loves the Lord with all her heart, mind, body, soul and strength. Ruth is a Church School teacher and regards this assignment as a privilege to be able to tend the hearts and minds of the children. Ruth is active in other ministries in the church, enjoys writing, and serves as an Assistant Editor of *Green Pastures*.

Joseph Thompson, former chef and printer, is from South Carolina. He has been a member of Second Baptist Church, Roselle, for two years. For years he felt drawn to the church but did nothing about it until he suffered a heart problem which brought home to him the need for God in his life. Today he is an active member of the Male Chorus and the Usher Ministry, and diligently is serving the Lord.

Reverend Barbara D. Turner is a resident of Roselle and a paraprofessional in the Roselle Public School system. She assists with the needs of special education students and loves them to the Lord as only she knows how. Reverend Turner loves the Lord and has been serving the needs of God's people for many years at Second Baptist. She is a Bible scholar, Armor Bearer, and avid sports enthusiast. Reverend Turner is a Chaplain for the United Chaplin International Worldwide Outreach, Inc., and a member of the Baseball Chapel Prayer Team. In addition to serving as Spiritual Advisor to several auxiliaries throughout the church, Reverend Turner is the Director of C.L.I.M.B Ministry, where she continues to help build stable lives by the power of God while embracing the vision of the Church. She also serves as Assistant Editor of *Green Pastures*.

Barbara Brigg Turner is the youngest daughter of the late Alexander Sr. and Lillian Briggs. She has been a member of Second Baptist Church for sixty years. She accepted the Lord Jesus Christ as Savior at an early age and understood the importance of serving God and His people. This legacy of service has been passed on to her children, grandchildren, nieces, nephews, and children in the Lord. Members of the church affectionately call her "Mother Turner" or "B.T." The ministries "B.T." is involved in include Pastor's Aide Ministry, the Mother's Club, the Floral Ministry, Missionary Ministry, Woman's Guild, and the Caring and Sharing Ministry which serves our homeless and displaced brethren. She also serves as pianist for The Nursing Home Ministry and is one of our Prayer Warriors. She is grateful to God for her family, friends, and the "K-Five", our wonderful Under-Shepherds — Pastor and Minister Margaret Moore — their children, and the household of faith.

Evonne Tyree and her husband, Bill are early retirees. They reside in Roselle, New Jersey. They have two sons, Minister Michael and Brandon. Evonne is a member of Second Baptist Church, Roselle, New Jersey, where she sings in the Mass Choir, the Praise Ensemble, and serves as President of the Women of Praise Choir. She is also an advisor to the C.L.I.M.B. (Christ Lives in My Body) Ministry and Treasurer of Pastor's Aide Ministry at Second Baptist. She renders solos of Christian music at her husband's family reunions that have been taking place annually for over 20 years. The Lord God is always at the base of each reunion weekend event. Most importantly, she loves the Lord and feels blessed by having the love of Christ surrounding her through loving family, church family, and close friends.

Minister Michael W. Tyree is a devoted servant of the Lord Jesus Christ and he implores all people to allow God to use them in whatever capacity God has purposed for their lives. Minister Mike believes that the current day Christian has been commissioned by Jesus to share the gospel with the world. He beseeches all Christians to live as 2 Chronicles 7:14 teaches and to operate under the power of the HOLY SPIRIT. Minister Mike is a Co-Chair of the Board of Trustees and is dedicated to serving the Lord. He desires to make a difference in the lives of children and adolescents by encouraging them to heed God's voice.

Deaconess Catherine Williams is a member of Second Baptist Church, Roselle, for thirty years. She is the wife of Joe Williams, and the mother of seven children. In addition to serving in the Diaconate Ministry she is actively involved in the Mothers' Club and the Marriage Ministry.

C.L.I.M.B. Ministry
Abide in me, and I in you. As the branch cannot bear fruit of itself, except it abide in the vine; no more can ye, except ye abide in me." John 15:4

The C.L.I.M.B. (Christ Lives In My Body) Ministry meets every Thursday evening with an emphasis on discipleship, evangelism, and fellowship for those between the ages of 13 and 18. In their weekly sessions, they discuss living their lives in the Lord through Bible study, spiritual enrichment sessions, prayer partner fellowship, chapel, movie night, and their annual sleepover. This ministry is directed by Reverend Barbara D. Turner who leads with her good examples, prayers, teachings, and encouragement. Members of C.L.I.M.B. look forward to reaching higher heights in Christ and lifting Him up higher and higher.

Second Baptist Church

200 Locust Street, Roselle, New Jersey 07203
http://www.secondbaptistroselle.org

Phone 908-245-7571

Rev. James E. Moore, Sr. Pastor

1890 – 2009

One Hundred and Nineteen Years of God's Sustaining Love.

Second Baptist Church, 200 Locust Street, Roselle, New Jersey, USA was planted in 1890 by a seven-member team of Christians with a vision and abiding faith in what God can do. Rooted and grounded in The Word of God, Second Baptist Church has grown, flourished and continues to bear much fruit to the glory of God.

Come and worship The Lord with us.

NOTES

NOTES

NOTES

Breinigsville, PA USA
20 January 2010
231064BV00003B/1/P